Andy Johnson. Ph.D.
Dept. of Psychology
Bethel University
3900 Bethel Drive
St Paul, MN 55112

Navigating
the Academic Career

Common Issues
and Uncommon Strategies

D1524748

Andy Johnson. Ph.D.
Dept. of Psychology
Bethel University
3900 Bethel Drive
St Paul, MN 55112

Navigating
the Academic Career

Common Issues
and Uncommon Strategies

by

Victor N. Shaw
California State University—Northridge

Information Age Publishing, Inc.
Charlotte, North Carolina • www.infoagepub.com

Library of Congress Cataloging-in-Publication Data

Shaw, Victor N.
Navigating the academic career : common issues and uncommon strategies / by Victor N. Shaw, California State University, Northridge.
pages cm
ISBN 978-1-62396-117-6 (paperback) -- ISBN 978-1-62396-118-3 (hardcover) -- ISBN 978-1-62396-119-0 (ebook) 1. Universities and colleges--Faculty. 2. College teachers--Employment. 3. Universities and colleges--Administration. I. Title.
LB2331.7.S53 2013
378.1'01--dc23

Printed in the United States of America

CONTENTS

PART IV

INTRODUCTION

Career making is a universal phenomenon in the modern and postmodern era. From the original need of earning a living, to the personal aspiration for self-actualization, and to the social requirement of answering one's calling in an earthly enterprise, career making has reached the surreal of producing and reproducing identity, status, and seemingly even immunity from the ultimate human fate, death (Baudrillard, 1988; Bland, Taylor, Shollen, Weber-Main, & Mulcahy, 2009; Engvall, 2003; Feldman, 2013; Gardner & Barefoot 2010; Hermanowicz, 2012; Nealon, 2012; Philipsen, 2008; Rhode, 2006; Rossides, 1998; Weber, 1930). The academic career, in particular, ensures that an individual pursuing it is socialized in a field of knowledge. One first learns to speak a specialized language known to the members of the field. One then formulates an agenda for advancement, presents one's ideas and findings, and engenders an autobiography of specialties, titles, honors, and tenure which may be memorialized and followed by other academicians beyond one's physical existence.

The sequence makes an ideal career pathway. In reality, although hundreds of thousands of people aspire wholeheartedly and work painstakingly for an academic career, not everyone is able even to gain entry to academia. Among entrants, not everyone is fortunate enough to triumph through competition to win a place, obtain a sense of identity, and become a figure of importance in the academic community. Many aspirants are eliminated along the academic career pathway, even just at the beginning of formulating a research agenda or locating an academic niche. Thus, making a career in modern and postmodern academia may not only pave the way toward self-realization of individual potentials and

Navigating the Academic Career:
Common Issues and Uncommon Strategies, pp. vii–x
Copyright © 2013 by Information Age Publishing
All rights of reproduction in any form reserved.

ambitions; it may also create a path for victimization and destruction of individuals (Bland et al., 2009; Clark, 2006; Elliott, 1996; Gardner & Barefoot, 2010; Goldsmith, Komlos, & Gold, 2001; Grant & Sherrington, 2006; Hermanowicz, 2012; Philipsen, 2008; Rhode, 2006; Schuster & Finkelstein, 2006).

In a broader social context, career making derives from modern mass production and division of labor (Feldman, 2013; Marx, 1967; Nealon, 2012; Paechter, 2001; Popkewitz & Fendler, 1999; Slaughter & Rhoades, 2004; St. John & Parsons, 2004). Mass production necessitates a knowledge enterprise to continually prepare personnel and supply software. The knowledge enterprise proliferates rapidly over time. It becomes so complex that it develops a division of labor within its own sphere. The division of labor in the knowledge enterprise results in borders among disciplines, demarcations among fields in a discipline, and designations of specialties in a field. A single specialty in a field may still be too large for a person to master within his or her lifetime. To maintain a specialty, a field, a discipline, and further the knowledge enterprise, individual academicians have to stay on one after another as if they were making a career of their own. However, in the sense that the knowledge enterprise serves the needs of mass production, glorifies the history of human triumphs over nature, and supplies means for individual socialization, academic career making contributes to the production and maintenance of the capitalist social process. In other words, it generates authority, ideology, and the mainstream, which in turn can belittle, devaluate, and repress individuals and their intellectual initiative.

This volume examines academic careers and career-making activities with respect to their main aspects, milestones, and general pathways. At a philosophical and epistemological level, a combinational approach is taken to provide academic professionals with individual, institutional, and contextual accounts of their careers and career-making endeavors. An individual account makes academicians think about what they do and how they might do it better. An institutional account makes academicians reflect upon the organizational environment in which they function and ponder what they might do to improve it. A contextual account connects academicians and their work to knowledge, the knowledge enterprise, and the larger social structure so that they know and understand the impact they and their career-making efforts have on themselves, academia, and general social processes.

At a pragmatic and practical level, this volume attempts to (a) generalize from existing career-making experiences, (b) conduct an informing and enlightening analysis of issues specific to career academicians, (c) offer useful suggestions for individual scholars, and (d) provide a reliable guidebook on scholarship and academia for the general public. Specifically, the volume aspires to (a) apply to scholars in all disciplines, not just liberal arts, engineering, or science; (b) appeal to faculty in all academic institutions, not just small-town teaching colleges or large-city research universities; (c) tackle all important issues a career scholar has to deal with in his or her scholarly life, not only teaching, research, service, and citizenship, but also education and reeducation, job search and job change, organizational employment, publication, presentation, application for grants and awards, and participation in academic associations; and (d) touch upon all critical stages a career scholar has to pass through in his or her academic journey, not only the start, but also the middle and the end.

With regard to suggestions and the way in which they are made, this volume does not treat any of its potential readers as a child as do many faculty guidebooks in the market. It does not intend to give any step-by-step instruction. It offers no-nonsense advice only on critical issues in career and career-making, such as researching, publishing, and managing departmental politics. Although issues are common, strategies suggested are uncommon, not the usual stuff of advice columns in publications such as *The Chronicle of Higher Education*. Also, different from other faculty guidebooks that hand out instruction in a "politically correct" way, this volume presents useful ideas straightforwardly and offers necessary guidance in an easy-to-access manner.

In content, this volume divides into four identifiable parts. Part I, composed of Chapters 1, 2, and 3, focuses on professional preparation. It examines education, degree, reeducation, job search, and job change. Part II, consisting of Chapters 4, 5, 6, 7, and 8, centers on organizational employment. It investigates position, research, teaching, service, and tenure. Part III, including Chapters 9, 10, 11, 12, 13, and 14, revolves around professional networking. It looks into publication, conference presentation, application for grants and awards, and membership in academic associations. Part IV, comprised by Chapters 15 and 16, rises above specific issues. It explores general career pathways and overall scholarly identity.

Each chapter includes two standard sections. Section 1 provides both a brief historical and a general contextual, from economic, political, and social to cultural, analyses of the issue to which the chapter is dedicated. Section 2 offers practical suggestions for career-making scholars to deal with the issue. Suggestions are specifically elaborated in organizational, disciplinary, and/or professional dimensions.

Overall, this volume shall interest graduate students, postdoctoral scholars, junior researchers, probationary faculty, and tenured professors as both a forum for theoretical reflection and generalization and a guide for doing and practice. Academic administrators and career counselors may also use it as a helpful resource or, better yet, as an inspiration for innovation and reform. For prospective academic career aspirants, significant others of academic practitioners, and the general public, the volume can provide an excellent glimpse into knowledge, scholarship, the academic profession, and the educational enterprise.

PART I

CHAPTER 1

EDUCATIONAL PREPARATION

The academic career begins with education. Education itself is a long process, constituting a significant part of the career pathway (Abel, 1984; Altbach, Gumport, & Berdahl, 2011; Bowen & Rudenstine, 1992; Butin, 2010; Davis & Parker, 1997; Dore, 1976; Eurich, 1981; Gardner & Barefoot, 2010; Gardner & Mendoza, 2010; Golde & Walker, 2006; Holley, 2011; Lee & Danby, 2012; Maki & Borkowski, 2006; Paechter, 2001; Shaw, 2002c; Sowers-Hoag & Harrison, 1998; Taylor, 2005; Tinkler & Jackson, 2004; Walshaw, 2012).

BACKGROUND AND ANALYSIS

The goal of education is to inculcate in prospective entrants basic values, common codes of conduct, established theories and methodologies, current debates, and recent developments of a discipline in particular and of the whole academic community in general. Compared to the time of Plato or to the Middle Ages when apprenticeship under a spiritual master for a few years was deemed enough to prepare a person for philosophical or theological undertakings, the education required for an academic career in the contemporary era can take as long as about one third of one's lifetime. First comes precollege education from kindergarten to twelfth grade, a standard socialization process assumed for common citizens in modern society. Then comes a 4-year undergraduate education, a general social requirement designed for middle-class employment and lifestyle under affluent capitalism. Next is a 3-year master's-level graduate education, where one either lays a foundation for one's academic pursuits or prepares oneself for business management, technical or professional jobs, and other high-paying employment. Master's-level education therefore serves only as a baseline for or a transition to the higher levels of training required for an academic career.

The standard for career academicians, for college and university professors, is doctoral education. Despite years of learning at precollege, baccalaureate, and master's levels, doctoral students still spend an average of 6 years to complete their work for a degree of doctor of philosophy or PhD. With this degree, they merely meet a minimum requirement of qualification for teaching and research in academia. In fact, as the academic labor market remains a strong buyer's market, the minimum entry requirement with regard to education and training shifts to an even higher level. More and more teaching and research institutions now tend to recruit only those PhD holders who have a few years of postdoctoral training and work experiences in other similar organizations.

In the process of academic career making, education plays the dual role of both gatekeeper and track-setter. As gatekeeper, education screens in only those who are able to survive its lengthy and pedantic procedure. An enrollee has to take many examinations and contests to prove that he or she has mastered all necessary knowledge and skills for academic undertakings in a specific discipline. In addition, one has to submit to a myriad of exercises and challenges to demonstrate that one has internalized all appropriate rules, codes, and distinctions for professional practice in the community of scholarship. It is known that students drop out of the educational process when they fail in major examinations in an academic subject. It is, however, not so publicized that students are forced out of educational programs because they are not willing to kowtow to their advisors or because they are determined to challenge an academic authority with regard to a substantive fallacy or an unprofessional practice. There are no sufficient conditions in knowledge acquisition and behavioral maturation. A career-making scholar can never proclaim that he or she has learned enough in or beyond school. Instead, one has to always connect oneself to the educational system for continuing learning and resocialization throughout one's academic career.

As track-setter, education predesignates what field or subject one is to delve into, what perspective or orientation one is to take, and what finding or product one is to turn out in one's academic career. It also preassigns where in the academic world one is to play one's role and build one's influence. Specifically, the institution from which one graduates and in which one finds one's graduate advisor and classmates predetermines what network one enters and how removed one is from the core of the academic community. A graduate under the apprenticeship of a prominent scholar from a leading department in an elite university has a totally different network waiting for him or her than one graduated from an institution deemed mediocre.

The faculty directory, which conventionally includes information about a faculty's graduate school and academic interests, showcases how graduate school sorts out academic hopefuls, feeding them into different institutions in higher education. In California, for example, graduates from elite institutions, such as Harvard, MIT, and Princeton, fill positions in elite schools, such as Stanford and Caltech, University of California (UC) campuses, and sometimes the California State University system. Graduates from leading UC campuses, such as Berkeley and University of California at Los Angeles, feed less prominent UC campuses, the California State University system, and sometimes community colleges. Graduates from UC campuses dominate the California State University system and major community colleges. It is rare that graduates from a less prominent UC campus take positions in leading UC institutions, much less in elite schools within the state.

One argument for the track-setting influence of graduate education is that graduates from top programs have undergone more rigorous training in fundamental skills and knowledge in a discipline and therefore possess a greater potential for significant contributions to the academic enterprise. There is, however, support for the opposite of this argument. That is, top graduate programs do not necessarily produce only high-quality students while lower ranking ones may be able to individualize programs for students and produce competent academic professionals. Institutionally, top programs are considered elite not so much because they produce first-rate students but rather because they have the best-known scholars on their faculty. These scholars are preoccupied with their own research and may be less likely to spend a lot of time with their students. The situation is further complicated by the number of students. Many top programs attract a large number of students in their graduate population. Another factor is that well known programs, as they stand securely at the top, may tend to care less about whether they turn out a few lesser quality products among a large group of good ones. On the other hand, lesser known programs are likely to be new and small; their faculty members are therefore highly motivated to prepare students with all necessary skills and knowledge for long-term growth in a discipline. Faculty members may spend more time on graduate advisement. Each graduate student, among the few in the program, may receive a great amount of supervision and scrutiny throughout the educational process.

As a result, graduates from some lower ranking programs may, in fact, be better prepared for work and contribution in academia.

PRACTICE AND SUGGESTION

Anyone who has gone through graduate school may wish he or she had done it differently. For those who plan to go and are currently sailing through graduate education, suggestions can always be precious and useful (Axelrod & Windell, 2012; Bolker, 1998; Bowen & Rudenstine, 1992; Bowen & Sosa, 1989; Butin, 2010; Ellis, 2001; Gardner & Mendoza, 2010; Gossett & Bellas 2002; Holden, 1991; Holley, 2011; McAlpine & Amundsen, 2011; Thomson & Walker, 2010; Tuckman, Coyle, & Bae, 1990; Walshaw, 2012).

Suggestion 1: Aim high at the best graduate school you can attempt with your existing achievements and resources. Graduate school lays the ground for your academic career. Graduation from a more prestigious program puts you in a more advantageous position to enter academia. Getting into a higher ranking program is more competitive. Once you are in the program, however, you may find you have more freedom, more positive references, more sources of motivation, more opportunities, and more resources than you would have in a less well regarded institution. Most important, you establish a resourceful network with faculty and fellow students, you develop a kind of elitist mentality and competitive spirit, and you set a generally high level of expectation, all of which may give you an edge over other competitors from less prestigious institutions.

Suggestion 2: Work with the most active and productive scholars in the faculty. It may be difficult to get hold of a higher achieving member of the faculty because he or she is preoccupied with his or her research agenda. A less productive faculty member, on the other hand, is likely to entice students by offering his or her insights about departmental politics. Unfortunately, entering students can be easily swayed by personal mannerisms and end up working under less achieving faculty. There are possible detriments when you are supervised by less productive advisors. For example, they may use students as political chips to gain advantage over their higher performing colleagues: "I have brighter students under my umbrella or I produce better students." They may hold unreasonable expectations and confront their students with unattainable goals: "I have never been able to write such well-structured essays for those high-ranking outlets. I now can only work hard to coach my students in the hope that they will fulfill my dreams and ideals."

Suggestion 3: Do what your advisors do while not necessarily doing what they say. It is obvious that there is a gap between what one says and what one does. In education, while most students are used to listening to their professors, the most powerful way of learning is still to observe, to be motivated by, and to emulate what a revered advisor is doing and has accomplished. Graduates from an elite school are able to achieve more in their career, oftentimes not because they have mastered a significantly higher level of knowledge, but rather because they have internalized a more merit-oriented mind set, from a more brilliant and accomplished faculty. In all graduate education settings, it is therefore important for students to go beyond instructional routines and overtures and to get down to the essence of what makes their professors effective and successful academic workers.

Suggestion 4: Do not change your area of specialization unnecessarily. Change is costly. It is wise to be patient in deciding on an area of interest in the beginning. It is unwise, however, to abandon effort in one area and to delve into a new territory in the middle of graduate training. Learning is a lifelong process for career scholars. You learn something from graduate school. Graduate school is your key to getting started in academia. It is not your once forever preparation for scholarly undertaking. Sail through your graduate training as uneventfully as possible. Do not take it as an opportunity to concentrate on a theory, a method, a procedure, or a technique. You will soon find out that you learn most on your own while at work.

Suggestion 5: Move beyond graduate training. Graduate education is a rite of passage into academic career. Professors as rite-presiders are poised to keep you fearful and overwhelmed by all those assignments, examinations, and requirements. Rise above surreal activities. Move beyond training protocols. Start working as a scholar. Conduct manageable research. Edit student journals. Explore funding sources, professional associations, and publication outlets. Present papers to professional conferences. Participate in national and international competitions. Write research reports and submit manuscripts to the academic media for publication consideration. With proper perspective and control, all these extra-curricular efforts will not only give you positive feedback on your graduate training, but also put you a few steps ahead of the game in your later career development.

CHAPTER 2

THE DEGREE

The degree marks admission to the world of scholarship. With a doctoral degree, one conducts research, teaches classes, and participates in academic debates as if these activities were taken for granted. Without a proper degree, however, one probably has to put out a disclaimer whenever one sets out to do something within the academic circle. In the structure of an academic career, the degree is a cornerstone to determine the scale and the outlook of the building that sits on it (Abel, 1984; Anastas, 2012; Bowen & Rudenstine, 1992; Bowen & Sosa, 1989; Cartter, 1976; Clark & Centra, 1985; Conley, 1997; Dore, 1976; Golde & Walker, 2006; Maki & Borkowski, 2006; Mullen, 2012; Noble, 1994; Pappas & Jerman, 2011; Taylor, 2005; Walker, Golde, Jones, Bueschel, & Hutchings, 2008; Webb, 2009).

BACKGROUND AND ANALYSIS

The degree is the end product of education. It carries all the information acquired through the educational process as well as all the commands held by the educational establishment.

The number of degrees shows the breadth of one's training and knowledge in academic subjects. In social presentation, one or more doctoral degrees, along with a few lower degrees, may create an impression that one is diversely trained in multiple areas. For example, one who holds a PhD in electronic engineering and a PhD in history may be considered as

Navigating the Academic Career:
Common Issues and Uncommon Strategies, pp. 9–14
Copyright © 2013 by Information Age Publishing

a prime candidate for research in the history of technology. One who holds a bachelor's degree in chemistry, a master's degree in physiology, and a PhD in psychology may be regarded as a promising scholar in substance abuse research. As far as lifetime productivity is concerned, however, multiple degree holders may not necessarily be in an advantageous position. They spend more years in school. Knowledge and modes of inquiry they learn from different disciplines or levels may lead to contradiction and confusion in their research choices. Most important, in an era of specialization, a discipline is likely to be dominated by those who settle in the core of the discipline, rather than by those who wander into border areas with other disciplines.

The sequence of degrees from lower to higher levels demonstrates the depth of training and knowledge one has gone through in scholarship. There are all-in-one discipline degree holders. They take the same or similar subjects from undergraduate, to graduate, and to doctoral studies. They obtain their bachelor's, master's, and doctor's degrees in the same discipline. Over years of learning, they may gain a firm grounding in the theoretical and methodological approaches developed in the discipline. There are multiple-discipline degree owners. They take different disciplines, one in college, another in graduate school, and still another in doctoral level studies. The degrees they hold show the sequence in their educational effort. For example, one obtains a bachelor's degree in mathematics, a master's degree in business administration, and a doctor's degree in sociology. This sequence in education may likely qualify the candidate for teaching in a business school. Likewise, one who has a BA in philosophy, a JD in civil law, and a PhD in political science may find placement in a law school. It is obvious that a cross-discipline educational sequence not only widens one's exposure to scholarship, but also deepens one's involvement in it.

The degree concludes education and neutralizes high with low performers in the educational process. One may not do well in a multitude of courses, retake major examinations, and struggle all the way in graduate school. But as long as one holds the degree in hand, the struggling achiever will be treated similarly to a stellar graduate in academic practice. As for productivity, high performance in school may not necessarily translate into more accomplishment in academic career. There are hundreds of cases where lackluster or rebellious students make brilliant or creative scholars. There are thousands of cases where model students fade into mediocrity later in their academic life. In fact, many successful scholars may well credit their career achievements to some unconventional ways of thinking they have developed from the time of being a student.

The degree serves as an identifier in professional networking. Within a department, having a PhD from the same university may be the primary reason why a kinship relationship is forged between faculty members, a political faction is developed, or a kind of loose alliance on issues is maintained. At a college- or university-level gathering, graduation from the same institution may bring strangers into warm and meaningful conversations. After the conversation, some of them may continue in their informal or formal contact. Across an organization, a community, or a region, alumni from a university may gather in association-chapter meetings, exchanging ideas and offering mutual support in academic work. Another occasion in which the degree often figures in importance is the academic meeting. An accidental greeting or casual conversation at the reception, by the registration desk, or at the end of a session may lead to in-depth relationships when the degree from the same institution happens to be mentioned as a reinforcer. Some mentors may use a meeting to take former students to a dinner or to attend an academically oriented activity. There are national and international meetings where organizers reserve a night or hold a place just for alumni get-togethers. Some ties can therefore be forged and developed over individuals' academic career.

The degree also carries specific social expectations. At the time of job search, a graduate from an elite university may be pressured to apply only to research institutions even though the job candidate is a little unsure of his or her aptitude for research. Academic advisors may explicitly say that they send letters of recommendation only when their graduates apply to universities that emphasize research. On the other hand, a graduate from a less elite university may be forced to apply only to institutions where the teaching load is heavier and research is less emphasized even though the candidate is prepared for and enthusiastic about serious research. Research universities in the market are likely to suggest, if only implicitly, that the candidate is not suitable simply because of his or her Alma Mater. Later in the career path, a degree holder is supposed to behave in a way expected by the university that conferred the degree. For example, a graduate from a little known university could create a surprise across a field if he or she makes an important breakthrough on a long unsolved problem. A degree holder from an ivy league institution could be held in contempt if he or she turns out products deemed in low quality or below the normal expectation. To emphasize the differential value and expectation inherent in a degree, academicians normally include the name of the degree, the year in which it was obtained, and the institution that conferred it in their curriculum vitae. Institutions also selectively focus on those essential variables to present information about their academic staff in the organizational directory or at public briefings.

The degree itself is considered an achieved status. Just as professionals in law, business administration, social work, or nursing proudly put JD, MBA, MSW, or RN after their name in official communications, academicians holding a doctor of philosophy (PhD) in their discipline expect to be honorifically addressed as Dr. X in social interactions and be accorded proper treatment in academic dealings. Academic institutions also use the percentage of PhDs in their faculty or staff as an effective measure to attract students, to convince funding sources, or to demonstrate their adequacy and competency in the world of scholarship. The doctoral degree has long become an established indicator in official statistics compiled by the government and academic associations.

PRACTICE AND SUGGESTION

Degrees are obtained in the early stage of an academic career. They settle in the bottom or background of one's scholarly identity or structure to influence how one perceives oneself and how one fashions one's academic adventure.

Suggestion 1: Walk out of the shadow of your degree. As soon as you finish your degree, you become an accepted citizen in the community of scholarship. Do not feel privileged if you hold your degree from an ivy league institution. Do not feel disadvantaged if you have the stamp of a lower ranking university on your diploma. Focus on your work. You will sooner or later be judged solely by your abilities, performances, and contributions. Another bit of advice is this: Overcome any bookishness you may carry with your degree. You are now a doer. Liberate yourself from any too rigid plan or schedule to read books or to perform some student-like routines. Follow your scholarly intuitions, gut, and senses. Put yourself in the mode of creation and production instead of reception and absorption. Still another stride to make is to take up new projects, set new agendas, and delve into new areas of inquiry. You may need to spend a year or so to conclude your degree-related work. Revise your dissertation into a book. Break your thesis down into several articles for publication in academic journals. Or improve some course papers for conference presentation or as book chapters. But do not keep digging where you were when you started work toward your degree. There are scholars who still write about the same thing 10 years after the receipt of their degree. They obviously do not make much progress in their career.

Suggestion 2: Obtain an MBA if you want to teach in business school. If you are in a discipline within social sciences or the humanities, you may want to work in a border area with business administration. Spend some time on an MBA. With the degree, you make yourself qualified to teach in a business school. In a time of economic booms when people are driven by economic rewards to the world of business, there is usually a shortage of faculty in MBA education. You can handily land an academic position on a university campus. Most important, you can add a significant amount to the salary you would normally make as a faculty in other disciplines. Apart from the mercenary motive, a stint in business administration may broaden your research horizon from your home discipline to such interdisciplinary territories as international trade, corporate deviance, business economics, conflict resolution, and organizational behavior.

Suggestion 3: Obtain a JD if you want to teach in law school. By the same rationale, you may want to supplement your PhD in a social sciences or humanities discipline with a doctoral degree in jurisprudence. JD is a master's-level degree although it sounds doctoral. Teaching in law school, you make more money. With money, you may free yourself more from the strain you typically experience in life with limited income from academic undertakings. You familiarize yourself with both the legal field and your original discipline. With cross training and exposure, you become a prime candidate for scholarly contributions in public policy, legislative process, and various social issues. Even in research methodology, you may combine your original disciplinary approach with case analysis and other characteristically legal procedures for fruitful and insightful results.

Suggestion 4: Obtain a professional degree if you want to run a professional practice. A professional degree may involve a degree in nursing, chemical dependency treatment, clinical psychology, social work, and other specialties. With a professional degree, you may obtain a state license to practice in an area of service or treatment. Practice can be a substantive complement to research. You have the opportunity to be in touch with clients. You gain the access to reach and handle different cases. The information you have gathered and the experience you have accumulated, when put in proper perspective, can be a never-ending source of inspiration for theoretical generalization and methodological development. The scholarly pursuit, under the mandate of your doctoral degree in a discipline, will also enlighten your practice, making you a more informed and sophisticated practitioner.

Suggestion 5: You need only one doctoral degree. MBA, JD, and professional degrees are master or lower level degrees. You may obtain one of them on your way toward or upon the completion of a doctoral degree, without significant investment. Unless you are totally burned out from one discipline into which you are forced by a doctoral degree, do not work on a second doctoral degree in a different discipline. Needless to say, do not attempt two doctoral degrees when you are in school. You need only one doctoral degree to be a legitimate member of the community of scholarship. It is simply a waste of time and energy to use another degree to knock open the door to another discipline. If you are interested in a new field, you can always make your expansion from your home discipline. For example, you are fascinated with psychology while you have your doctoral degree in sociology. You can pursue your research in the framework of social psychology. When you make a name within the two disciplines, you may eventually find you are welcomed by both psychology and sociology.

CHAPTER 3

JOB SEARCH AND CHANGE

Education is a necessary condition for making a career in academia. It follows an academician all the way along his or her career pathway. It is not, however, a sufficient condition. A prospective scholar who has fulfilled all educational requirements has yet to locate an academic institution in which he or she can earn a living and make connection to the established academic mainstream (Abel, 1984; Barnes, 2007; Bentley, Coates, Dobson, Goedegebuure, & Meek, 2013; Bowen & Sosa, 1989; Brada, Stanley, & Bienkowski, 2012; Cartter, 1976; Clark & Centra, 1985; Dore, 1976; Formo & Reed, 2011; Heiberger & Vick, 2001; Hume, 2010; Shaw, 2000; Vick & Furlong, 2008).

BACKGROUND AND ANALYSIS

The search for a job is part of an academic career because the position found places one in a work environment that may determine one's productivity, contributions, and quality of life. The search is not part of academic effort because it just meets a survival requirement. If he or she did not have to, no scholar would like to engage in job search, a disturbing distraction from serious academic work.

In general, job search provides one with the first opportunity to assess one's situation for a real-life academic adventure. After years of schooling, one has achieved something by obtaining a doctoral degree in a subject area. But most of one's properties are still ascribed: What age range one falls under, what racial and ethnic group one comes from, what gender category one belongs to, what school one graduates from, and whom one works with as mentor. The last two characteristics are partially achieved rather than ascribed because it takes efforts to enter any graduate school and a school of great prestige in particular. As wholly achieved properties, such as the dissertation, a number of articles in print or accepted for publication, and a few courses taught, are somewhat sketchy for beginning academicians, they may soon realize that it is important who you are or where you are from in the community of scholarship, just as it is important in the world of the mundane.

Specifically, one can learn a few lessons through job search. First, one can immediately know whether one's advisors are genuinely supportive. Do they write glowing or business-as-usual recommendations? Do they give honest advice on where one should apply for one's first job? Do they send their letters of recommendation in a timely fashion? Do they warn that they can send only a few letters on one's behalf? Second, one can immediately observe the change in attitude and behavior by academic insiders. As student, one receives advice and encouragement from one's advisors and other seniors in the discipline. As soon as one's student chapter is closed, disciplinary insiders begin to look at one as a competitor. They no longer treat the candidate with condescension. They do not show kindness and support either. Third, one can have a critical taste of rejection from academia. One sends out a group of application letters with sincere hopes. One is soon pounded repeatedly by negative responses. One begins to understand that the academic world is not always a land of realizing dreams. Fourth, one learns to take a business approach toward the academic career. One is given a telephone interview, a campus visit, and a job offer. One manages one's impression, negotiates with job grantors, compromises on expectations, takes advantage of one's situations, and maximizes gains. Fifth, one develops a definite sense of reality about oneself regarding all of one's ascribed and achieved features. How much is one welcomed as a male or female, a gay or lesbian, a minority or majority member, a person of color or noncolor, a native or nonnative speaker, and a person of young or middle age? How much is one appreciated as a graduate from an elite versus a nonelite school, a student of a renowned versus an ordinary scholar, and a junior academician of considerable versus minimal achievements? Finally, one learns to accept the fact that academic work is a profession and that academia is a market place. Throughout the entire job-search process, one walks out of one's idealized view of scholarship and academia, plunging into the reality of competition and struggle for survival. One begins to realize that engaging in academic work is not only to pursue a noble goal but also to secure a source of income. One begins to understand that in an academia where market forces reign, one fails or succeeds not only by one's own endeavor but also by unexpected luck or misfortune.

If first job placement hinges basically upon ascribed characteristics, later job change is to a large degree prompted by achieved properties. While everyone has to look for a first job, not a great many academicians ever change their jobs. There are several reasons for the general lack of job change among academic professionals. First, most scholars land ten-ure-track positions. It takes years of effort to be tenured with an institu-tion. One loses one's years of service for tenure when one leaves the institution. One is not likely to regain full service credit for tenure upon joining a new institution. Second, most tenured scholars tend to stay with their guaranteed jobs because few academic institutions are willing to grant tenure to a once-tenured scholar from another institution. Who wants to exchange his or her tenured job for an untenured one? Which institution would follow its competitor's rules in offering someone tenure without applying its own standards for tenure? Third, academicians are judged primarily by scholarly contributions rather than years of service. Scholars who have been in long years of service are not necessarily strong "comeback kids" in the job market if they do not have adequate contribu-tions on their records. One simply looks unworthy when one has a long history of service and a short list of achievements. Fourth, academic cre-ativity and productivity are essentially uncertain and unpredictable. While an institution is interested in hiring a candidate because of his or her existing accomplishments, that candidate may not always feel so confi-dent about his or her future efforts and fortunes in a new organizational environment. Finally, the academic profession is relatively guarded from market forces. Scholars who are devoted to their academic pursuits are likely to put up with difficulties and setbacks in mundane life. As a result, there is far more old-fashioned commitment and loyalty to employment than benefit-driven or gain-motivated job change and switch among aca-demic professionals.

Despite a generally low level of change, academicians do look for and take up new jobs after their initial placement. There are typically three types of job change among career scholars. One takes place in the first several years among new entrants. New people may change their jobs rel-atively frequently because (a) they have difficulty in adapting to scholarly work in general and assimilating to an academic institution in particular; (b) they maintain contact with their advisors and feel free to ask them for letters of recommendation; (c) they have yet to realize the importance of time and tenure in academic life or simply wish to explore the world for a few years; (d) they switch from research-centered or elite to teaching-ori-ented or nonelite programs and vice versa as they know more about what they want to do and can do as career scholars; (e) They still look new and promising; and (f) hiring institutions tend to bet that first-time job defectors from another institution are more likely to stay with them than those brand new graduates who have never had any formal employment experience. Another job change involves job opportunities related to academic employment. There are people who fall off the conventional academic track. They may conclude their premature scholarly career once and forever. They may land governmental, industrial, service, or counseling jobs related to their academic training and pursue freelance or applied research with or without formal connections to their discipline. There are people who move from applied fields to the academic mainstream. With inspiration from their practice-related jobs, they may become more productive scholars. There are people who move from affiliated research centers to established academic departments within an institution. With grant experiences from funded research, they may be better positioned to gain tenure and to serve the university community. There are also people who change their jobs because of marriage and family obligations. Still another job change falls upon those who have developed an attractive research record as well as an extensive scholarly network within and outside their discipline. They are enticed to join a department, lead a unit, or develop a program with higher salaries, more power, and richer resources. At the personal level, such job change signifies recognition, reward, and upward mobility in the academic career. Among institutions, it points to the competitive edge private, research, and elite universities often have over their public, teaching, and nonelite counterparts.

From a historical and systemic point of view, an academic job market takes form and sustains itself when educational institutions continually turn out qualified job seekers, existing job occupants frequently switch employment institutions, and academic employers routinely change their personnel. In the distant past, no job market existed when some reflective or investigative personalities self-taught to be academic masters and cultivated close apprentices to be their followers in a subject or institution. As universities were opened from place to place, there used to be a brief period of time when academic departments desperately hunted for eligible candidates to fill their faculty vacancies with bachelors, masters, or even no-degree practitioners. A similar situation may appear in new areas of inquiry where qualified scholars have yet to be trained by first-generation explorers. But the academic job market as a whole in the contemporary era has long and consistently featured a high supply of prepared applicants and a low availability of appropriate openings. Educational institutions are well established and prepared to produce doctoral graduates. No institution would volunteer to cut programs or eliminate itself because some of its graduates are not able to secure academic jobs. Some programs may even capitalize on the oversupply of academic candidates to expand and to maintain its scale. Doctoral degree holders then have to go overseas, enter nonacademic sectors, such as industry and government, or retreat to part-time teaching or postdoctoral research as they fail to crack open the front door to academia. There may be seasonal, periodic, regional, or discipline-specific loosening when the number of applicants comes more nearly into balance with the number of openings. Oversupply, however, will stay long and steady as a landmark feature in the academic job market. In a sense, it reflects how employment standards or educational levels move up in both academic and nonacademic sectors. The academic sector begins to retain only postdoctoral trainees for its own use while the nonacademic sector takes more and more doctoral graduates from it.

PRACTICE AND SUGGESTION

Suggestions can be readily found in guidebooks for job search and change (Barnes, 2007; Cartter, 1976; Cotten, Price, Keeton, Burton, & Wittekind, 2001; Formo & Reed, 2011; Gray & Drew, 2008; Heiberger & Vick, 1992; Hume 2010; Lyson & Squires, 1978; Mullen, 2012; Rodmann, 1995; Shaw, 2000; Sowers-Hoag & Harrison, 1998; Vick & Furlong, 2008). From a career point of view, one may just focus on five dos and don'ts.

Suggestion 1: Do prepare a comprehensive curriculum vitae but do not show everything to everyone. A comprehensive curriculum vitae should divide into major sections, including education, employment, publication, presentation, professional service, reward, and association. Under each section, you list all your specific and specialized experiences and accomplishments. The all-inclusive vitae is the backbone of your application. You start with it but do not present all of it when you prepare a particular application package. It is a crime to make up something you do not have on your record. But it is your discretion to include or not to include something you have done in an application. While it is difficult to read people's minds and predict how you are evaluated, it is important to follow some general rules that always hold. For instance, it may be disadvantageous to you if you include a lot of nonacademic publications or purely communal services when you apply to a top research university. People there may question: Is this applicant being carried away by his or her nonacademic interests? On the other hand, it may hurt more than help you if you include too many publications and professional engagements when you deal with a primarily teaching institution. People there may wonder: Can this applicant be serious about teaching?

Suggestion 2: Do explore the whole market but do not apply everywhere. Exploration of the whole market means that you gain access to all job listings in all sources of advertisement in your discipline. There may be statewide, regional, national, and international associations as well as sectional or topic-specific groupings. Each organization may include job openings in its newsletter, website, journals, or special employment bulletins. At its annual meeting, it may offer employment services through which you meet with prospective employers. With a systematic knowledge of the whole market, you not only know what is available, where to start, and when to apply, but also develop a general assessment of market balance between demand and supply as well as your own prospect for employment. Do not, however, apply to many places even when you know there are many openings for which you feel qualified. First, you need only one job. You may be able to negotiate a higher salary when you have a few offers from which to choose. But negotiation with focus on financial gains may not necessarily reflect well on you. Also, you may sometimes have to come back to a place you once rejected. Second, it is better to remain unknown than known in the job market. If you are turned down once by a place, you are not likely to be accepted by the same place for a second time. Third, the world is small. You reduce your own chance of employment if you are somehow known to be a desperate, unselective job seeker.

Suggestion 3: Do aim high at the best institution but do not take a job that could make you fail. You ride in a boat. You stay on top when your boat sails on high water in a rising river. Most intellectuals aim high in their job choices. In a prestigious institution, you are likely to gain better access to resources and opportunities, to receive higher levels of support and encouragement, and to interact with more creative and productive peers. You may feel that it is easier to succeed in an environment that is designed to make you succeed. However, a generally supportive environment and a basically motivated individual do not necessarily combine to make automatic success. Individuals act differently in the environment. Environment impacts upon individuals differently. You may fail on your first job in a competitive and demanding institution. Failure can be devastating. It shakes your confidence. It dampens your vision of the future. It shadows your whole academic career. Practically, people cheer you on when you move from a lower to a higher institution. They may cold-shoulder you when you look for a way out of your rather high place. In other words, you may find it rather difficult to just find a job when you come back to the market.

Suggestion 4: Do keep an eye on the job market from time to time but do not change your job with unnecessary frequency. Change is a motivator. Expectation for change can make you stay active, productive, and current with your discipline. To benefit your upward career mobility, it is important to monitor the job market from year to year so that you know what is available. For example, you work in a teaching university and you want to join a research institution. You may keep an eye on job situations among research universities and see whether your credentials render you any competitive edge in that segment of the job market. Change, on the other hand, is disruptive and costly. You may lose some years of service credit for tenure. You may have difficulty unlearning your past experience and adjusting to a new environment. The contrast between old and new institutions can be dispiriting, especially for untenured scholars. You are close to being in the role of a "mother-in-law" in your old institution no matter how dissatisfied you feel about that role. You are a "daughter-in-law" in your new institution no matter how hopeful you are in that position.

Suggestion 5: Do prepare for the unexpected but do not let job change take you to a downward career movement. Life is unpredictable. So is your scholarly career. You may begin with a rather mediocre institution. You work hard, smart, and productively. You eventually sit in an honorable position in a prestigious university. There are, however, unfortunate scholars who take a downward slide in their career. They start off at a reputable institution. They gradually ride down the slope either because they do not produce anything or because they do not get along with people. They may move from higher to lower ranking, from research to teaching, and from national to regional institutions. They may change from tenure-track to nontenure and from full-time to part-time positions. They may eventually exit from academia into other fields. As far as the job market is concerned, do not be enticed and fooled by the availability of jobs in the market. You can change jobs. But the best thing to do, when you already have a job, is oftentimes to keep your job. There might be operational difficulties, occasions of setback, and spots of conflict. But as you stay on, problems can go away by themselves or turn into something positive. Be patient. Let time take care of difficulties. An inexplicable desire for change may put you in a restless mood. Do not let it take you to a downward spiral in your academic career.

PART II

CHAPTER 4

ORGANIZATIONAL EMPLOYMENT

Institutional affiliation is another necessary condition for an academic career. Just as in education, where not everyone passes various hurdles to reach the doctorate, not every degree holder is able to locate and solidify an institutional base in the academic world (Altbach, Gumport, & Berdahl, 2011; Bentley, Coates, Dobson, Goedegebuure, & Meek, 2013; Bianco-Mathis & Chalofsky, 1999; Bok, 2003; Bolman & Gallos, 2011; Brada, Stanley, & Bienkowski, 2012; Brown-Glaude, 2008; Clark & Lewis, 1985; Coiner & George, 1998; Gosling & Noordam, 2006; Greenwood & Levin, 2001; Hermanowicz, 2012; Jedding, 2010; McCaffery, 2010; Newman, Couturier, & Scurry, 2004; Readings, 1996; Rhodes, 2001; Shattock, 2003; Toren & Moore, 1998; Weingartner, 1999; Weingartner, 2011; Wildavsky, 1989).

BACKGROUND AND ANALYSIS

Institutional affiliation remains at the center of an academic career. First, the institution provides a secular job by which a career-making academician earns an income to support himself or herself. In the era of social differentiation and organizational employment, it is rare for a scholar to be able to do serious academic work and build a respectable career by

Navigating the Academic Career:
Common Issues and Uncommon Strategies, pp. 25–31
Copyright © 2013 by Information Age Publishing

either taking a nonacademic job or selling his or her academic products directly to a buying market. Social perception dictates that a career professional falls under the general division of labor and belongs to a systematic operation of the academic enterprise. Personal limitation does not allow for frequent switches among different states of mind and modes of activity. A career-making scholar relies upon an academic institution for his or her survival needs and for work in a specialized area of inquiry.

The fact that career-making professionals depend upon colleges or universities for employment income makes the quality of an academic career conditional on the level of support afforded by the institution. As it is known, faculty members in elite schools and leading research universities not only receive better salaries but also are better equipped for supplementary income through grants and consulting. Faculty members in less prestigious institutions, on the other hand, have to engage in off-semester teaching to increase their usually meager salary. The worst situation is that of postdoctoral scholars who receive only fellowships as their major source of income. To make ends meet, they either work on someone else's project or commute to different campuses for part-time teaching. Difference in the level of income often translates directly into qualitative difference in scholarly activity and output. Better-paid scholars have more time to do research, show higher productivity in publication, and enjoy more visibility in scholarly influence. In contrast, lower paid academic professionals spend more time on teaching, have less time for research, turn out fewer publications, and are hence more likely to fall into obscurity in the academic community.

Second, the institution provides an indispensable environment in which career-making academicians develop ideas, produce scholarly products, and prepare them for academic circulation. Academicians need to use books, journals, documents, and other academic materials in libraries, special collections, or archives; they need to work in laboratories if they practice in a discipline that depends upon experimental work; they need to attend professional seminars, disciplinary workshops, and thematic conferences; they need to consult or debate with colleagues, students, and other qualified participants; and they need to obtain secretarial or technical support and utilize computers, copying machines, and other modern research tools. In small or remote institutions, academicians may not find most of their needed references in a small library on campus or in the whole area. Interlibrary loans offer some relief but have various constraints. One has to file paperwork or pay money; one has to wait and can keep a loaned item for only a short period of time; and oftentimes by the time of the arrival of a requested item, one has already lost momentum for any serious use of the item in research. In institutions with a lack of academic stimulation, people may shun each other on scholarly matters; not many brownbag activities, seminars, speeches, or conferences are available on campus; and various constraints are instituted to limit access to information from the outside, to discourage contacts with colleagues in other institutions, and to limit attendance at professional conferences elsewhere. Obviously, career making depends upon institutional support; and support afforded by an institution varies according to its scale, mission, reputation, and resource. Differences in institutional support can translate directly into differences in scholarly productivity. It is a totally unfair game for a career-making scholar in a resource-impoverished, academically backward college or university to compete for academic recognition with his or her counterpart in a resource-rich, academically stimulating institution.

Third, the institution connects academic career aspirants to a disciplinary establishment in particular and the academic mainstream in general. It grants academicians legitimacy in conducting scholarly activities and assigns them specific tasks in research, service, and teaching. Just as education gives them stamps of proof for entry into the world of scholarship, institutional affiliation provides academicians with "drivers' licenses" to function in the modern academic enterprise. The academic enterprise is a well-differentiated and well-organized operation. Questions lie under defined subjects. Subjects fall into recognized fields. Fields belong to established disciplines. Disciplines are institutionalized in academic organizations through centers, departments, and colleges. In order to raise meaningful questions, develop sensible solutions, and make recognizable breakthroughs in academic matters, individual scholars have to enter an academic organization, work in a specific division, and specialize in a particular domain of activity or territory of interest. In other words, academic tasks are socially defined, assigned, and executed through organizational establishments. No matter how many ideas, insights, and talents they have, individual academic aspirants may only fall into obscurity or deviance if they fail to place themselves properly in institutions in the academic enterprise.

The importance of institutional affiliation in keeping academicians in the academic current and mainstream was long witnessed even in the beginning of the modern academic era in the discipline that is least dependent upon institutions. In the early 1800s, philosopher Ludwig Feuerbach soon found himself dismissed from the academic currency after retreating into countryside living. In the ever-changing 21st century, how far can a philosopher go if he or she stays out of an academic institution without access to the literature, the logistical support, and the oftentimes institutionally or socially created and maintained debates on issues? It is needless to say a scientist who depends upon the library, the laboratory, the grant, and the community of science formed and supported within and among academic institutions.

Finally, the institution serves as a screening and sorting mechanism for social placement. Within the academic community, it determines how academic professionals develop their self-concept and self-image, how they are identified by other academic organizations and practitioners, and how they as well as their activity are coded into the knowledge enterprise. There obviously exists not only a system of knowledge in terms of subject, field, and discipline, but also a hierarchy of academic practitioners according to their position, seniority, and institutional affiliation. An academic institution grants positions, rewards, and honors to individuals who are affiliated with it. An individual and his or her academic products are then identified and labeled, in almost every occasion, by his or her affiliated institution as well as the position and honor he or she has earned from it. It is natural for editors, funding agencies, and other academic community members to use one's institutional affiliation as a primary basis to make decisions regarding one's fundamental interests: whether or not to give one's manuscript, research proposal, or speech serious consideration for publication or funding. On a regular university campus, students and the faculty keep rushing to seminars conducted by guest professors from Harvard, Oxford, Cambridge, and other well-known institutions even though they are often disappointed by the actual substance gained in such seminars. The academic brand names are just so eye-catching that they seem to work in the academic unconsciousness. At a typical academic journal, the editor has access to information on a manuscript's authors and their institutional affiliation, and makes the first decision whether to reject an article submitted without peer evaluation or to send it out for review. Who knows what difference institutional affiliation makes when a journal editor evaluates two similar articles, one by a senior professor of an Ivy League university and the other by a junior member of the faculty at a small liberal arts college or an urban comprehensive university whose primary mission is known to be undergraduate instruction?

Outside the academic community, institutional affiliation provides an academic professional with social legitimacy, identity, status, and impression in interacting with friends, relatives, neighbors, and other members of a community. Social legitimacy concerns one's qualification to speak and publish in academia as well as one's deservedness of the kind of social expectation and respect accorded to the academic profession among all other different occupations in society. The fact that one works for a locally known academic institution as a researcher or professor automatically removes any reservation in the mind of local residents about one's legitimacy as an academic professional. Social identity concerns how one is identified in social communications. For example, one is called "Professor X" if one holds a professorial position in a university. Social status determines how much respect and what kind of treatment one receives from one's community and social network. Neighbors may address an academician with an honorific title when he or she exercises in the community park, dines in local restaurants, or shops in neighborhood stores. Friends and relatives may look up to an academician for advice and suggestions on matters of importance to them. Finally, social impression confers a general social image by which academicians are perceived and treated by others in the community. It is a generalized social property they develop and possess out of their legitimacy, identity, and status pertaining to their occupational pursuits.

PRACTICE AND SUGGESTION

To function productively and comfortably in an institution, an academician needs to be open-minded, to take suggestions, and to be flexible to accommodate different ways of thinking and acting by various parties in his or her surroundings (Bianco-Mathis & Chalofsky, 1999; Bland, Taylor, Shollen, Weber-Main, & Mulcahy, 2009; Chu, 2012; Cyr & Reich, 1996; Dews & Law, 1995; Feldman, 2013; Hermanowicz, 2012; Jedding, 2010; Joughin, 1967; Mullen, 2012; Philipsen, 2008; Piper, 1992).

Suggestion 1: Focus on your own work. You are a scholar. You are not only judged by colleagues in your institution, but also evaluated by peers in your discipline. Be attentive to what your colleagues say and what your institution expects. But do not be dictated to and carried away by their suggestions and requirements. Formulate your own research agenda. Pursue your own scholarly interests. Develop your own academic career. Do not abandon some topics or subjects, avoid some theories or methods, shun some conferences or publications, or give up some efforts or quests, just to please your colleagues or just to follow some mandates by your institution. As long as you focus on your scholarly duty and put the best into your work, you will eventually be understood and recognized.

Suggestion 2: Be careful about your immediate leader. You begin as a small player in a large institution. Your immediate leader evaluates you. His or her evaluation can set the tone for all the other evaluations to be done about you at the higher levels. While most academicians are conscientious professionals, there are always a few individuals who are less capable of making objective and rational decisions in their job functions. In an extreme case, your immediate leader may even influence students about your teaching effectiveness, persuade senior colleagues about your research worthiness, or set up a generally repressive environment to make you either suffer or flee. It is totally unpredictable what kind of environment you will plunge into and what kind of leader you will have to deal with. One thing for sure is this: be careful about your immediate leader. He or she can make you a gem of your unit. Or he or she can interrupt you in your planned journey no matter how much you have accomplished and how hard you work. In the meantime, be optimistic; merit, justice, wisdom, appreciation, and universal love for humanity shine high and bright over small dark and dirty pockets of mediocrity, discrimination, foolishness, envy, and hatred.

Suggestion 3: Maintain proper distance from your colleagues. There are different approaches toward colleagues. The two often talked-about extremes are these: your colleagues are your friends because you draw inspirations and support from them; and your colleagues are your enemies because you compete with them for limited resources within your unit, institution, and discipline. The reality is likely to be this: your colleagues are neither your friends nor your enemies. They are just people you work with in an institution and discipline. An important issue in working relationships is, then, distance. On the one hand, you need to be close enough to your colleagues so that you can listen to them, take their suggestions, evaluate their work, and help them with their problems. On the other hand, you need to be distant enough from your colleagues so that you can respect them, leave them with sufficient freedom and comfort to pursue their own interests, appreciate their contributions, and maintain your own autonomy in your work.

Suggestion 4: Be aloof over and away from local politics. Politics permeates where people live and work. Academic institutions are not exceptions. In fact, political divisions and confrontations become so intense in some academic units that one side may not be on speaking terms with the other for years. When you join an institution, you may be approached by one faction to join its force against the other. Be calm. Be cool. Stay neutral. Politics is deceptive. Politics may promise you gains and advantages if you do well or do better than the average in your institution. Politics may render you hope and support when you struggle to salvage your tenure and job. Politics can be disruptive. You could lose a lot of your valuable research time and energy to oftentimes useless political fights. Politics can be poisonous. Your scientifically comprehensive mind could change into an ideologically biased one. Politics can be addictive. You could be carried away from your academic endeavor by seemingly forceful and refreshing activities and changes in politics.

Suggestion 5: Be unmoved by and unconcerned with material gains and losses. Working in an institution involves rewards, benefits, salaries, and promotions. As an academic employee, you need to deal with a full range of material gains and losses in your life. You join an institution with an impressive record but you are not given a benefit package commensurate with your achievements. You may achieve more than the average member of your department but you receive a smaller salary increase than most of the other members in your unit. You may be denied promotions while those who have accomplished less in the same period of time are promoted. Your salary may stay low, even lower than some newly arrived colleagues in your unit. Your salary remains flat while some of the colleagues in your cohort have orchestrated several increases with appropriate stakeholders in different levels. All these material inequalities happen from place to place and from time to time. They can create a sense of unfairness and injustice in your mind. Are you able to be unmoved by and unconcerned with all and each of them so that you can focus on your work and do the best of your work?

CHAPTER 5

POSITION

Academicians earn positions through individual efforts. The position earned will in turn determine what academicians do and how much they do in their career-making endeavors. Academic beginners usually earn their position by the doctoral degree they achieve from the educational process. In their junior position, they may only do certain things and are likely to face various constraints even in their limited areas of work. Seasoned academicians, on the other hand, earn their positions either by years of service or by substantive contributions. In their senior positions, they may perform a variety of tasks and are likely to receive assistance in a wide range of functions. The unequal distribution of tasks and responsibilities leads directly to the unequal share of benefits and rewards, differentiating academicians into various stages and statuses in their career-making pathways (Alstete, 2000; Beckham, 1986; Bianco-Mathis & Chalofsky, 1999; Bright & Richards, 2001; Brown-Glaude, 2008; Clark, Fasching-Varner, & Brimhall-Vargas, 2012; Dulmus & Sowers, 2012; Finkelstein, Seal, & Schuster, 1998; Gornitzka, Kogan, & Amaral, 2007; Jedding, 2010; Leaming, 2003; Licata, 1986; Long, McGinnis, & Allison, 1993; Lucas, 2000; McCabe & McCabe, 2010; McCaffery, 2010; Schuster & Finkelstein, 2006; Tierney & Bensimon, 1996).

BACKGROUND AND ANALYSIS

There are different positions for academicians to acquire and take in various domains. Employment-related positions may include temporary versus permanent, part-time versus full-time, tenure-track versus tenured, probationary versus regular, and junior versus senior jobs or titles. Entering academicians may start with temporary and part-time jobs to accrue experience. When they land permanent, full-time jobs, they are likely to be in junior, probationary, or tenure-track positions. Seasoned scholars, on the other hand, are likely to be tenured in senior positions. Although they have full-time, permanent jobs, they may take part-time, temporary positions, such as consultants and visiting professors or researchers, to diversify their work and life experiences. Temporary, part-time positions, in this regard, have totally different outlooks and effects for entering and seasoned academicians. For the former, they are uncertain, exploitative, humiliating, and indicative of low status. For the latter, they are assuring, complementary, and status enhancing. In fact, they serve for many senior career scholars as an indicator of recognition, reputation, and influence.

Institution-granted positions clearly mark the rank, seniority, and status achieved by academicians in their career-making process. In universities, there are lecturers, senior lecturers, and professors or assistant, associate, and full professors. In research organizations, there are junior and senior associates, analysts, or scientists. These titles or positions have specific responsibilities and rewards associated with them. Academicians have to meet specific requirements or complete certain years of service with certain amount of work to move from lower to higher levels.

Association-designated positions come from professional associations to which career-making academicians belong by their subject interest, geographical location, individual background, or other characteristics. Associations are formed by practicing academicians to exchange ideas, advance common interests, and make a social impact. They serve members in their academic pursuits. They also provide members with opportunities to gain status. The presidency and vice presidency of associations are usually reserved for scholars of outstanding achievement. In addition, associations may use their newsletters, journals, and annual meetings to solemnly award members with such honorific titles as distinguished career contributor and scholar of the year. For many academicians, taking an official position or being recognized with a formal title by their association represents an important milestone in their academic careers.

Discipline-based positions may include various voluntary and honorary roles that support the life of a discipline. There are editors, associate editors, journal reviewers, and book reviewers who control and maintain the flow of information within the discipline. There are grant reviewers and project evaluators who decide the distribution of resources among practicing academicians in a field. There are conference organizers, session moderators, and panel discussants who perform on public stages in a subject area. There are also pioneers, founders, inventors, and discoverers whose names are affixed to a concept, theory, or method in a field and are celebrated, honored, and glorified from time to time in the discipline. Obviously, assuming a secular position as editor, reviewer, or organizer in a discipline enhances one's visibility, influence, and status. Being deified as a pioneer, founder, or classical figure may even extend one's academic career beyond the limit of one's lifetime to the status of a contributor to the evolving progression of human knowledge.

It ought to be pointed out that the position achieved in a particular domain not only determines the nature and scope of responsibilities and rewards one receives within that domain, but also affects the way one participates in the activities of other domains. For example, an academician who holds an assistant professorship in his or her college or university is not likely to assume the presidency in a well-recognized academic association or to be on the editorial board of an influential journal in a discipline. Also, there are overlaps and reinforcement effects among positions in different domains. Being recognized by an established academic association as a distinguished scholar may significantly reinforce one's professorship in one's home institution, bringing the honored individual tangible benefits from a one-time award to a permanent increase in salary.

PRACTICE AND SUGGESTION

Taking positions or positioning in an employment organization or an academic association is the most important issue a scholar has to deal with in his or her academic career. There are thousands of academic practitioners. There are many approaches to positions and positioning. It is obvious that there are a myriad of suggestions as how to perceive and assume different roles and responsibilities in one's employment and professional environments (Bland, Taylor, Shollen, Weber-Main, & Mulcahy, 2009; Buller, 2010; Chu, 2012; Feldman, 2013; Gardner & Mendoza, 2010; Hermanowicz, 2012;McAlpine & Akerlind, 2010; McCabe & McCabe, 2010; Philipsen, 2008; VanZanten, 2011).

Suggestion 1: Enter your position as a conforming objector or an objecting conformist. By common sense, most people enter their job as pure conformists. They follow insiders, listen to members of the old guard, learn rules, familiarize themselves with procedures, and strive to become part of the crowd. From a psychological and organizational behavior point of view, however, mere conforming or conformity is not necessarily the most effective or beneficial way to start your job. You are a lot better off if you begin as a conforming objector or an objecting conformist. As a pure conformist, you make your boss or senior colleagues feel you are not someone to be worried about or concerned with. They know you will take it if they throw something at you. As an outright objector, you make your organizational stakeholders feel you are a troublemaker to either work with or get rid of. Sooner or later, you will see you have nothing to object to because you are objected to or ejected out of your job. In between as a conforming objector or an objecting conformist, you may put yourself in a far more advantageous position for the greatest possible reward. For example, as a conforming objector, you fight discrimination, challenge unfair treatment, denounce politicking, avert factionalism, and object to poor performance, all with a conforming attitude. You do not necessarily look for negative issues. But when they occur in your sight, you take them to the appropriate authority for some kind of remedy, following proper institutional procedures. You leave to your leaders or senior colleagues an impression that you are a strong willed individual, you respect authority only when it is impartial, and you honor institutional practice only when it is rational. With that impression, stakeholders in your job are likely to give it a second thought when it comes to making a judgment about you and your fundamental interests.

As an objecting conformist, you listen, observe, and make an effort to fit into your institution, but with caution, questions, and reservations. You ask for explanations and clarifications when you encounter obvious ambiguities and irregularities. You suggest change and modification when you see a more effective or rational way of solving a problem. Gradually, you make your senior colleagues and leaders feel you are a careful and conscientious person and they can trust you with your unique yet helpful perspectives. On the matter of an interest essential to your career, they may consult with you in advance or attempt to convince you when a decision is made.

Another interesting contrast to notice is starting a position with some solvable problems versus with some impressive deeds. Beginning with some worry-invoking problems, you make your senior colleagues and leaders feel you need help and assistance. You take the opportunity to accept their advice and make appropriate improvements. By the time when a critical decision is in order, you are already a well-rounded and well-qualified candidate for upward movement. The availability heuristic works for you as information available in the most recent time weighs more heavily than what occurred far in the beginning. Most important, you make your senior colleagues and leaders feel they have contributed to your rise to a higher level. On the other hand, when you start off with an impressive performance, you may set a higher bottom line for your later work. You are fine if you keep performing well and do more. You can be questioned or even criticized for slower or declining performance, however, if you do not keep pace with your past records. The availability heuristic can turn against you because information about your most recent situation may easily make your senior colleagues and leaders develop an impression about you as a person not "getting better."

Aside from practical pros and cons, being a conforming objector or an objecting conformist may put you on track for breakthroughs, unique contributions, or overall excellence in scholarship. In science, you create, discover, and innovate only when you question, challenge, and object to existing theories, paradigms, or practices. You participate, contribute, and leave an impact only when you respect, follow, and conform to basic scientific principles, methods, or procedures.

Suggestion 2: Focus on your position. It is obvious that you should focus on your job and do the best you possibly can. But you should be aware of an unconscious human tendency to deviate from duty and shun serious responsibility inherent in the job. As an academician, an important duty is to do research and share research findings with the community of scholarship. Believe or not, that is often the very thing you attempt to avoid every day. You search for shelters where you feel safe and comfortable from research. The most common shelters where you, as a trained scholar, feel comfortable to hide from research are in the areas of service and teaching. You engage in service because you feel you offer your expertise for a good cause. But you fail to realize or refuse to admit that some services you provide can be better performed by secretaries and that you could use your expertise for something far more important. You spend time unnecessarily on teaching to the point that you actually exploit your students for their valuable time and energy. You ignore the basic fact that students can learn more from exemplification than from preaching and more from identification than from face-to-face interaction. You look for excuses by which you rationally and reasonably explain why you skip research today and tomorrow. Excuses may vary from visiting a barber's shop, depositing a check in the bank, buying an advertised item from the store, and fixing a flat tire, to attending a sick relative. You make pledges, one after another, to yourself that you will go back to fieldwork, laboratory, experiment, or writing as soon as you clear up all those nonresearch concerns in your mind or finish all those nonresearch tasks in your hands. Day by day, you know there is never a time when you are totally free from all those secular concerns and matters. A realistic reaction, therefore, is to do something now and do something every day. There are good days and bad days. But if you understand your scholarly mission, know and dare to overcome all the negative currents within and without yourself that keep you from pursuing your dream, and do your job now 1 day at a time, you will be able to accomplish something in your lifelong journey in the land of academic inquiry and discovery.

Suggestion 3: Take a secondary position only when it comes logically from the primary one. Aside from the natural tendency to avoid your duty, there are various callings and opportunities derivable from your rightful job as a scholar. Being a practitioner in your discipline, you may be invited to serve as a manuscript or grant reviewer, to sit on an editorial board, or to edit a journal or a monograph series. Being a member of your association, you may be elected to become an executive secretary, a regional representative, a chapter convener, a program organizer, a vice-president, or even the president. Being a faculty member in your department, you may be voted into the position of chair, associate chair, graduate chair, or personnel committee chair. These seemingly secondary positions are directly related to your primary position. They demand time from you, but they may also bring a wide range of tangible benefits to you in your academic career. Although most academicians make an effort to vie for career-enhancing secondary positions, you may want to take a conservative approach instead. First, do not strive for it. When you fall into a position by a fluke, you are not likely to gain as much respect and influence as you are entitled to by the very position. You may be seen as a joke, a swing, or a puppet in some situations. Second, take such a position only when it comes to you naturally. It is natural that you assume the position of chair or associate chair in your department when you become a full professor. You need to think twice if you are cheered into the presidency of a professional association, even if it is regional or marginal in scholarly activity, when you have yet to establish yourself in a field or discipline. Third, perform your duty in a secondary position without serious interference with fundamental goals and responsibilities for your primary position. Always remember you will be judged ultimately by the achievements you make in your primary position. Fourth, do not feel you have been judged negatively when you lose a secondary position. You are always a scholar, an active and productive scholar, whether or not you are a journal editor, whether or not you are a department chair, and whether or not you are an association officer.

Suggestion 4: Keep a low profile. By commonsense wisdom, you hide from the public scene as much as possible when you do not do well or are judged as being only average, but let the dust fly high when you do well, far ahead of the normal pace of progress. But to be unique and productive, you should always keep a low profile. A low profile helps you stay on track with what you are determined to do, preventing you from being carried away by superficial or external praise, recognitions, awards, or honors. Most important, you avoid unnecessary scrutiny, trivial criticism, and even malicious attacks from those who judge you, who compare themselves with you, who are jealous of you, and who dislike you. Although academia is probably cleaner and perhaps more moral than other parts of the world, discrimination, envy, bigotry, and even hatred are still common sins committed by and against scholars. You would be childish and naive if you think everyone will cheer you on or trumpet your success if you prove yourself a genius or a superstar in academic undertakings. Instead, you should remain especially careful, cautious, modest, and collegial when you are one of the most popular professors in your department, when you publish more than anyone else among your colleagues, and when you have millions of grant dollars at your disposal.

Suggestion 5: Do not become an unscrupulous political opportunist. You stay long enough in your organization. You are senior in rank. You are experienced in relationships. You have multiple connections with the rank and file. You feel confident, comfortable, and convenient to talk to the chair in the department, the dean in the college, the chief in the union, the president of the university, and other stakeholders in the system. How do you then relate to people who are new, young, inexperienced, and lower in ranks? Do you knock at their doors, telling them not to do this and that? Do you stop them on the road, asking a favor from them or suggesting that they should do certain things? Do you intercept them in a professional meeting, reminding them of your seniority, superiority, and influence? More commonly, do you keep department secretaries working late for you, ignore junior colleagues' phone calls or email messages, or make a big fuss in the department meetings? Do you spy on junior faculty in their teaching? For instance, do you ask students how a newly arrived faculty conducts his or her class, suggesting that you have some kind of judgmental power over the faculty? Do you attempt to manipulate personnel process, broker a deal between disputing parties, or influence one side regarding its view on the other? If you do, you should confront yourself with one simple warning: "Do not be an unscrupulous political opportunist!"

In another scenario, you are productive in research activities. You are successful in securing funding and career-enhancing services. You feel you are smarter than anyone else in your department. Do you look down upon your less active, productive, and successful colleagues in the bottom of your mind? Are you rude to them? Do you ever make derogatory comments about them? Do you ever suggest to some of them that you would put their name on your publication or enlist them in your project should they call you "Uncle Superstar" or do you some favor? Do you feel you deserve more attention in a social gathering than anybody else? Do you feel everyone should pay homage to you at a ceremony in your honor? If you do, you should educate yourself about one simple truth: "Your personal success is not your ticket to manipulate, bully, and boss people."

CHAPTER 6

TEACHING

Teaching is an assigned task involving a time schedule, a classroom setting, and a student audience. To academicians who work in the university, teaching may be the only responsibility in which they can directly see and feel immediate reactions from an external force or authority. Students make complaints when professors fail to show up in class. Administrators take actions when students complain. Because teaching is situational and involving, some academicians, especially those who are not able to properly perceive and pursue research, often mistake it as the only duty they can intelligently handle in their academic career (Bain, 2004; Baldwin & Chronister, 2001; Bianco-Mathis & Chalofsky, 1999; Bland, Taylor, Shollen, Weber-Main, & Mulcahy, 2009; Buller, 2010; Chu, 2012; Fairweather, 1996; Gardner & Mendoza, 2010; Hermanowicz, 2012; Kalman, 2007; Lang, 2010; Lattuca, 2001; McAlpine & Akerlind, 2010; McCabe & McCabe, 2010; McKinney, 2013; Nilson, 2010; Philipsen, 2008; Shaw, 1999, 2001a, 2001b, 2002a, 2002b; Silverman, 2001; Sweet, 1998; VanZanten, 2011; Young & Shaw, 1999).

BACKGROUND AND ANALYSIS

Teaching, in essence, is a lively process of enlightening students with facts, ideas, logic, and reasoning, and, hopefully, changing those who are taught. But some outcomes of teaching can crystallize into measurable deeds in an academician's career. Statistically, for example, one can trace

Navigating the Academic Career:
Common Issues and Uncommon Strategies, pp. 41–48
Copyright © 2013 by Information Age Publishing
All rights of reproduction in any form reserved.

and record how many courses one has taught, what one teaches by subject, and where one teaches by institution; how many students one has taught in class, how many students one has advised in one-on-one settings, and what percentage of one's students graduate and further develop an academic or professional career; and what distribution one has in scores from blind student evaluations, how many times one is nominated for awards by students or peers, and how many awards in teaching one has actually received from recognized sources.

More substantively, a few academicians, upon establishing themselves as almost godly figures in a field or discipline, may be able to instantly turn their teaching into power and influence. Every word of theirs counts. Some of their faithful and thoughtful students carefully record their lectures, edit them into volumes, and publish them after the academicians' death. The practice started at the time when academic apprenticeship was a norm of training for new scholars. It continued over time but has become less and less common in modern and postmodern era. With the reality that mass production has long replaced apprenticeship in education, academicians in contemporary time can expect to be recognized for teaching only after they have realistically established themselves through publication. In the most likely scenario, a well-known academician attracts students from different places to study under his or her mentorship; some of his or her students achieve considerable visibility in the academic community and are able to publicly credit their success in some degree to him or her as a source of inspiration in formal media; and toward the end of his or her life, if he or she continues producing creative ideas and insightful thoughts through teaching and if he or she is unable to organize those ideas and thoughts in publishable format by himself or herself, some of his or her students may take action in recording them and preparing them for possible publication at a later time. Being publicly acknowledged by famous students in formal media is certainly a record of accomplishment or a deed of success in teaching for an academician. It is a matter of achieved honor and privilege when his or her lectures are recorded, edited, and published by students before and after the end of his or her academic career.

To fully understand the significance of teaching in the career structure of an academician, however, it is necessary to go beyond individual deeds and records to see how teaching impacts knowledge, the knowledge enterprise, people, and the society. First, teaching spreads knowledge. Although it does not create knowledge, teaching cultivates prospective knowledge creators and prepares them for formal knowledge production. Effective teaching saves students time and energy. Students may, in turn, use saved time and energy for more creative work. Inspirational instructors expose problems, raise questions, suggest routes of exploration, and provide direction. Students may be encouraged and enlightened to discover new interests, acquire new attitudes, and explore new avenues for endeavor in the process of learning. In some sense, it is legitimate to claim that you create knowledge whenever you pass on knowledge.

Second, teaching changes people and their lives. Students come to school for a variety of purposes, depending upon their age, race, profession, and socioeconomic status. Young people attend school to prepare themselves for entry into the labor market. Mid-career professionals take content courses to update their knowledge and build credentials for upward mobility. Senior citizens participate in classroom activities to renew their connection to society and enrich their mind with information and technology. For immigrants and the new generation of many deprived social groups, education provides them means to overcome their circumstance and to enter a new way of life. Through teaching, academicians generally assist people to achieve their goals and realize their dreams. In particular cases, one may be able to personally relate to some students and see how one changes their life through advisement, classroom instruction, or role modeling.

Third, in the university setting, academicians obtain their compensations primarily from teaching. A professor is paid, literally, for teaching students. Without students, there is basically no need for professors and there are no sources of income for scholars working in universities. In the spirit of pragmatism, an academician should obviously approach teaching as a serious duty on a paying job. Every time one goes into the classroom, one should ask: What do I have to offer my students? Every time one receives a paycheck, one should ask: Do I deserve it?

Finally, teaching feeds back on research. Scholars often use their classes to test preliminary findings and ideas. They benefit from student reactions and critiques in the refinement of their work. It is common that professors conduct a seminar or graduate class as a testing ground for their experimentation, book contract, or other endeavor. There is also widespread use of student labor and talent in research projects presided over by professors. In a subtle way, students serve for many ivory-tower scholars as links and bridges to reality, the future, and life. It is only fair to say that teaching is two-way traffic: Academicians learn from students when they teach them.

PRACTICE AND SUGGESTION

Teaching is experiential. Every instructor has his or her own unique strategies and tactics for classroom performance. Included in the following are five common issues an instructor may want to address and take a position on in his or her academic life (Bain, 2004; Bianco-Mathis & Chalofsky, 1999; Buller, 2010; Fairweather, 1996; Gardner & Mendoza, 2010; Hermanowicz, 2012; Kalman, 2007; Lang, 2010; McCabe & McCabe, 2010; McKinney, 2013; Nilson, 2010; Philipsen, 2008; Shaw, 1999, 2001a, 2001b; Silverman, 2001; Svinicki & McKeachie, 2011; Sweet, 1998; VanZanten, 2011; Young & Shaw, 1999).

Suggestion 1: Have a barrel when you give a bowl of water. The old Chinese saying emphasizes the knowledge base you need to establish when you teach. Having a solid and broad knowledge base, you can make proper selections and offer what is most relevant, important, and significant to your students. You can provide your students with a context in which they relate one issue to another, laterally, multilaterally, and structurally. You can offer your students a background upon which they make connections to the past, the present, and the future. As an academician, you are likely to exhibit two tendencies toward knowledge in teaching. On the one hand, you feel you know so much more than your students that you do not take serious interest in expanding, upgrading, and updating your knowledge. This happens frequently in general education, lower division, and even some upper division classes for undergraduate students. On the other hand, you assume you cannot possibly know more than your students that you do not make an enthusiastic effort to analyze, explain, and synthesize knowledge in a subject. This often occurs in graduate seminars, group sessions, and workshops for graduate students, mid-career professionals, and fellow academicians. To overcome both tendencies, you need to understand that knowledge is not a given. It changes. It is subject to interpretation and application. To lower level students, you may focus more on specific facts, concepts, theories, methods, or technical skills. To higher level students, you then need to demonstrate the complex process of analysis, rejection, confirmation, application, modification, and development regarding knowledge on a substantive issue. In any case, you always need to act in teaching upon an ever evolving knowledge system you actively maintain in your academic career.

Suggestion 2: Treat your students with care and respect. Your relationship with students is not one of equality. You have power over your students by the position you hold as instructor. Power may help you keep order in class. But it does not necessarily facilitate learning. A conscientious instructor should make an effort to defuse the sense of control and fear students may have about him or her. The instructor should do everything possible to make students feel comfortable about the instructor and feel good about themselves in class. The truth is this: They do well when they feel good about themselves; and they do not do well if they feel bad about themselves. There are two critical actions you can take in maintaining a learning-facilitative relationship and creating a performance-inducing class environment. First, you care about students and their learning. You take time to talk to them during office hours, before and after class, over the phone, and through the internet. You find words to cheer them up when they are sick, sad, and subdued. You recognize their efforts, progress, and achievement while you offer them comments, suggestions, and directions for improvement. Second, you respect students and their choices in learning. You thank your students when they raise questions, offer comments, hand in assignments, or take the initiative to suggest or organize certain class activities. For example, you may tirelessly say "thank you" when each student turns in their test in a large class. The "thank you" you say to them can serve as a recognition, a validation, and an appreciation from you as the instructor. In class discussion, you never embarrass a student by immediately, directly, and publicly pointing out that he or she is wrong with a comment offered or a solution suggested. Instead, you always help students manage any possible negative situation in classroom and, if possible, turn it into a positive experience of learning for the whole class.

Suggestion 3: Never fall into an argument with your students in or out of class. There are two possible argumentative situations you may fall into as an instructor. One is on issues in course content. Students may challenge you on your presentation, explanation, or interpretation of facts, figures, people, concepts, theories, or methods in a subject. The other is on grades you assign for class performance. Students may dispute with you regarding your judgment and judgmental standards on required class activities. No matter whether you emerge as a nominal winner or loser, arguments can only disrupt class, poison your relationship with students, and erode your confidence in teaching. It is therefore necessary to take preventive measures to avoid, contain, or change potentially argumentative situations with students. On the matter of issues, you first need to resist your own temptation to use the classroom as a personal forum to sell your own ideologies. You go to your class as an objective presenter of existing knowledge in a discipline. You let students know what your positions are, if you have your own, among an array of different ideas. Second, you need to provide a context for any challenging view raised by students. Within the context, students may automatically place their dissent in proper perspective. Third, you need to acknowledge the value of the challenge your students bring to an issue. You are not a housekeeper of the discipline or subject you teach. It, however, gives students a sense of validation when you say something about their effort in the name of science or on behalf of your discipline. Fourth, you need always to withhold your judgment on what students say and do in class. Observe it as a taboo in teaching: Never make your students look stupid. Instead of proclaiming that they are dead wrong when they are really wrong, you may say "it is a different way of viewing or handling the matter" or "it is common for people to take this route." Finally, if you indeed make a mistake, you need to be courageous enough to admit it and take appropriate action to correct it.

Regarding grade disputes, there are both strategic and tactical things you can do to keep matters under control. Strategically, you need to provide a clear and detailed description of class requirements in the syllabus. You may make general comments, provide grading rationale, and emphasize common mistakes made by the class before you hand out test results to students. Before you meet with a student disputing your grade, you spend time to review the student's tests, exams, or papers and figure out the most appropriate responses you will use to address his or her concern. Tactically, you do not address individual concerns in class. You give students sufficient cooling-off time when you make an appointment to see them. You highlight their achievements and progress. You turn their attention to the future by showing what they can do to improve performance. In general, you need to be firm with the decision you make out of your conscience and academic standards.

Suggestion 4: Be a source of inspiration rather than an authority of manipulation. In the position of professorship, you may not be aware of your tendency to manipulate or to exhibit manipulative behavior toward students. For example, to scare off students for a class you desire to keep small for your comfort, you may order half of a dozen expensive textbooks and make a long list of course requirements. To make time for a conference trip or your family vacation, you send your class to the library for literature review or to the field for data collection. To save your voice, you divide your class for group discussion, where students actually talk about weather, traffic, hot topics in mass media, or their personal habits. To shirk your duty as an instructor, you send your teaching assistants or graduate students to run a class. More creatively, you make your students present course content or engage in oftentimes aimless questioning-answering sessions so that you can sail through a class with ease and comfort. All these tricks are used by professors day after day and from class to class. They not only compromise the quality of education students obtain from the university, but also erode the integrity of the profession these professors live by.

As a practitioner, you can always do your part to reverse a pattern of behavior you deem inappropriate or inadequate. In teaching, the best way to connect to students is to take the position of students and exemplify rather than impose what they need to learn. Regarding course requirements, you tell your students stories about what you did when you were a student. You show them what you pursue and attempt to accomplish in research. You share with them your writings and publications. You avoid making any assignments you yourself could not complete satisfactorily or setting any standards you yourself would not be able to live up to. In offering advice on graduate school, professional choice, and lifestyle, you should avoid any tendency to impress students with your knowledge about a field and your connections to people in the field. You should also resist any temptation to convince students about a particular option you are personally in favor of. Instead, you should provide background, present context, compare options, and encourage different choices. As far as your work style is concerned, you should realize that students emulate professors in out-of-class behavior as much as they learn from professors in course content. You should be punctual in starting and concluding a class. You should be prompt in responding to student inquiries and in returning graded assignments. You respect students in class. You never miss a class. All these acts and deeds influence students as much as, if not more than, your explanation of concepts or theories in a subject course.

Suggestion 5: Explore new ways of teaching but do not be carried away by trendy practices. Course contents change. Students change. Social expectations and university requirements change. All these change agents dictate that you, as an instructor, change, not only in knowledge structure, but also in pedagogical style. To transmit knowledge to students effectively, you need to constantly and continually explore new ways of teaching. For example, how do you stimulate students to read course materials? How do you motivate students to share their ideas and experiences in class? How do you encourage students to put their findings and ideas into words in a research paper? How do you inspire students to do research and participate in academic dialogue in the form of professional presentation and scholarly publication? Innovations can be conceived and implemented in various fronts, from course design, examination, lecture, and class participation to grading, in order to achieve some of those goals.

In the meantime, you need to stick to the basics of teaching. No matter how innovative or effective a new method of teaching can be, there is essential academic content that can only be learned by students through appropriate preparation, hard work, and adequate intelligence, and can only be taught by instructors with proper background, serious effort, and sufficient wisdom. You take the initiative to explore new ways of instruction. You remain open-minded and embrace fashionable teaching methods when they come your way. But you also should be assertive and firm with those approaches and techniques that work for you and the students, even when they appear to be old-fashioned. Most important, you should make an effort to resist being carried away by trendy practices in teaching. For instance, some of your colleagues may rally students, administrators, and even politicians to advocate new modes of instruction, such as using a learning community, active learning, and service learning. Some of your colleagues may advise you to draw from students and replace lectures with class presentations and discussion. You may always listen to different opinions and examine different practices. But when you decide to adopt a particular way of teaching, you need to know and understand that the rigor of learning can be severely watered down by seemingly relevant activities inside and outside the classroom and that you fail to perform your duty in instruction if you do not or cannot inform students about reality or their experiential learning with theory or analytical understanding.

CHAPTER 7

SERVICE

There are essentially three dimensions in academic life: teaching, research, and service. The purpose of research is to generate and refine knowledge; the purpose of teaching to synthesize knowledge and pass it from generation to generation; and the purpose of service to relate knowledge to reality and apply it to improve the quality of life. In a sense, each dimension of academic life is equally important and valuable to human survival. However, there exists an institutional prescription of priority and limit for practicing academicians. Most institutions engage in research and/or teaching. Academicians working in those institutions naturally prioritize their activities in accordance with their institutional mission. Few institutions are set up as service organizations where working academicians take service as their overriding priority. As a result, there has formed a tradition among academicians that places service in a far less important position than teaching and/or research (Bland, Taylor, Shollen, Weber-Main, & Mulcahy, 2009; Bolman & Gallos, 2011; Buller, 2010; Chu, 2012; Clark, Fasching-Varner, & Brimhall-Vargas, 2012; Crookston, 2012; Dickeson, 1999; Fairweather, 1996; Goldsmith, Komlos, & Gold, 2001; Hamilton, 2002; Hermanowicz, 2012; Hunt, 2012; Macfarlane, 2007; McCabe & McCabe, 2010; Philipsen, 2008; Tierney, 2006; VanZanten, 2011).

BACKGROUND AND ANALYSIS

Service, as perceived and pursued by the majority of academicians in their institutional context, fulfills two important functions. One is citizen-

Navigating the Academic Career:
Common Issues and Uncommon Strategies, pp. 49–55
Copyright © 2013 by Information Age Publishing
All rights of reproduction in any form reserved.

ship. Academicians run committees, review papers and grants, organize meetings and discussion groups, voice concerns and opinions, and participate in various routine activities within their institution and discipline. By taking charge as responsible practitioners, they demonstrate the value of self-governance, promote the spirit of community, and maintain the life of their institution and discipline. In any typical university, there are committees, task forces, or policy groups at department, college, and university levels. Committees, task forces, or policy groups may deal with recruitment, performance evaluations, student awards, faculty incentives, academic grievances, educational resources, library acquisitions, technology, administration, community relations, and various other issues. Members of the faculty serve on committees, task forces, or policy groups, usually outside their teaching and research responsibilities, without any compensation in addition to their regular salaries. In all academic disciplines, there are manuscripts to be reviewed, grant proposals to be evaluated, conference programs to be assembled, meetings to be organized, newsletters to be circulated, journals to be edited, monographs to be published, associations to be maintained, and other academically related business matters to be attended to. Scholars spend a great deal of their time and energy on these service functions, often without monetary benefit and reward. There is no doubt that academic institutions, disciplinary associations, and the whole community of scholarship would cease operating should all their members shun voluntary good-citizenship service beyond regular paid job duties.

The other function is application. Academicians apply their knowledge and skills to the real world, offer advice, training, and direct assistance to people in need, and improve general spiritual and material conditions in the larger society. For instance, a medical scientist may run to the aid of an ailing neighbor. He or she may stop in traffic to attend the injured before the arrival of official rescuers. He or she may aid children in other countries in programs such as "Doctors without Borders." A criminologist may sit in a court hearing to offer expert witnesses. A psychologist may speak to the mass media about parenting and family life. A chemist may sit on the board of a local water treatment company to provide scientific advice. A civil engineer may testify in the city council about waste management across local districts. A sociologist may join a neighborhood committee to voice an opinion on various social issues. A social work scholar may volunteer in a public housing project for senior citizens to contribute observations and ideas to the management. In all these service activities, academicians may be paid for their time and effort, or they may not be given any compensation at all. They may be selected or invited because of their fame or specialty. They may step in out of their individual willingness. But one thing in common is that they apply knowledge to meet specific needs or solve practical problems in the real world. To the neighborhood, community, and society in which they live, academicians exemplify good citizenship when they apply their knowledge and skills to effect positive social change.

Taking a somewhat academically ethnocentric point of view, academicians may divide service into two categories: professional and community services. Professional service centers on academic activities that promote an academician's standing in his or her discipline. Specifically, it includes such activities as reviewing manuscripts, editing journals or monograph series, evaluating grants, organizing conference programs, leading panel discussions, presiding over scholarly exchanges, editing newsletters, maintaining email networks, serving on association committees, and becoming association officers. Academicians work on professional service activities under certain circumstances. By reputation, they are invited to serve as editors or grant evaluators, or elected to become association presidents or vice-presidents. Out of individual willingness, they volunteer to be manuscript reviewers, session conveners or discussants, and association treasurers or secretaries. Within a personal network, they answer calls by former or current advisors, colleagues, or friends to sit on editorial boards or program committees, or serve in some assistant positions for disciplinary associations. Professional service benefits academicians in different ways. It assists academicians to progress in their home institutions. Most academic institutions take into account service contributions in personnel decisions. It provides academicians with a forum to express their ideas or a network to spread their influences. Editors and association presidents can use service positions to reinforce their already achieved influences by way of publication. Finally, service motivates academicians to stay on the academic track, making their due contributions to scholarship. Most academicians serve their discipline in awe of academic giants and their scholarship. In service positions, they observe and learn how the academic process takes place and how academic celebrities rise from the majority of ordinary academicians. They are therefore stimulated, even inspired to continue in their own academic endeavors.

Community service, on the other hand, may originate from an academician's professional affiliation or specialty but does not necessarily advance that individual in his or her professional development. As far as activities are concerned, community service can range from serving on a departmental scheduling committee, a college personnel committee, or a university committee for student complaints and grievances, and serving on an advisory board for a community organization, a private business, or a level of government, to appearing on a news report, a talk show, or a documentary to offer expert opinions. Academicians engage in community services for important reasons. First is to fulfill an institutional requirement. As a full-time faculty member of an institution, academicians are expected to perform community services at department, college, and university levels. Service may be assigned by institutional authorities or won through open competition. Because questions about service quality and the extent of service can be raised in the personnel process, academicians may have to actively seek service opportunities in addition to a passive acceptance of service assignments by their supervising figures. Second is to gain insight, solidify a position, and expand influence. In their home institution, academicians serve in order to obtain a general understanding of how their institutional system works and take specific opportunities to strengthen their position in the system. In their communal and social environment, academicians serve to extend their presence and influence from work to life, from organization to community, and from academia to the larger world. Third, and less important, is to make money and win fame. Academicians may be compensated for their services when they sit on the advisory board of a public or private agency or serve as expert witnesses in court proceedings. They may even become famous if they are frequently featured in the mass media on specific issues.

How does an academician codify service into his or her autobiography of career and career achievements? There are essentially two approaches: outcome-oriented and activity-based. In an outcome-oriented approach, an academician looks into the result of his or her service. The questions one asks about one's service are these: What marks do I leave, what impact do I have, or what difference do I make in the lives of the people I serve, the culture of the institution in which I work, and the scholarship of the discipline in which I specialize. However, since outcome is difficult to measure in the flux of change within an institution, community, or discipline, most academicians opt for an activity-based approach. They record all the services in which they engage in their career pathway and take pride in just being part of their community, institution, and discipline through service.

PRACTICE AND SUGGESTION

As a free service provider, you need to overcome your tendency to downplay the seriousness of your service. You need to know and understand that what you do in your service position may have a significant impact upon an individual, a group, or an organization (Ackerman & Coogan, 2010; Bland, Taylor, Shollen, Weber-Main, & Mulcahy, 2009; Bolman & Gallos, 2011; Buller, 2010; Crookston, 2012; Fairweather, 1996; Goldsmith, Komlos, & Gold, 2001; Hamilton, 2002; Hermanowicz, 2012;

Hunt, 2012; Ledoux, Wilhite, & Silver, 2011; Macfarlane, 2007; McCabe & McCabe, 2010; Philipsen, 2008; Tierney, 2006; VanZanten, 2011).

Suggestion 1: Serve in your specialty. You may receive a wide variety of service calls and requests in your academic career. You need to be selective, definitely saying no to some while actively seeking opportunity for others. The best selection criterion is your specialty. When you serve in your specialty, you offer what you know and do best to the people or organizations you serve. You are not likely to make mistakes in your service functions. You distinguish your service as well as yourself if you are one of only a few specialists who are capable of performing the service. Most important, you have the opportunity to validate your training, test your knowledge, sharpen your skills, expand your experience, and forge possible relationships for collaboration, all within your area of specialty.

Suggestion 2: Serve to enhance your academic career. You do not have to be noble and unselfish when you engage in service. You may establish your own goals and set your own agendas while serving others. For instance, you may clearly state to yourself: "I review manuscripts because I want to see what is available in the forefront of knowledge, including new areas of inquiry, new methods of analysis, new modes of theorizing, and new forms of presentation." Practically, you may say in your mind: "I want to gain a little more insight into the peer review process, what a manuscript looks like at the time of submission, how an editor gathers and interprets comments from reviewers, and how comments are incorporated into revision. With a better understanding of peer review, I can do a more adequate job of writing and submitting a manuscript for review." Similarly in other service functions, you may seek realization of various career ambitions of your own: increase visibility, expand influence, accumulate experience, and prepare for advancement. For instance, you begin with some heavy-duty service as a local representative or a sectional committee member at your disciplinary association in the hope that you someday take the helm of the whole organization for one term or so. You run for the presidency of the faculty senate at your university because you aspire to become an administrator within the system.

Suggestion 3: Serve in areas where you are qualified. Because you offer your service for free, you may not face any careful scrutiny in your qualifications by the organization you serve. You may be called for service just because you have a PhD degree, are a tenured faculty member, or are a full professor. The voluntary burden of proof, as far as qualification is concerned, then ironically falls upon you as a responsible service volunteer. To serve your organization, discipline, and profession, you need to make sure you are qualified for the service you volunteer to perform. For instance, you may nominally qualify to review a manuscript in anthropology by the doctoral degree you have in anthropology or the professorship you hold in an anthropology department. But do you substantively qualify for the service if you have not published anything in the past 5 years? You may be eligible to serve on a personnel committee by the full professor position you secure in your institution. But are you actually qualified to make critical judgments on your colleagues in research, teaching, and service if you yourself demonstrate nothing but mediocrity in all three areas? Obviously, you may do a great disservice to your organization, discipline, and profession if you enter into service without substantive qualifications.

Suggestion 4: Serve with conscience. You take service credit when you put your name on a committee, a board, a team, or another service position. Because most service takes place in group settings, you may follow a group without any serious work. You may just give your nominal approval without ever showing up in group meetings. For instance, you sit on a graduate student's dissertation committee. You follow the chair of the committee. When the chair sounds supportive, you pick up a few points here and there in the thesis to demonstrate how ready the candidate is for the oral defense. When the chair sounds demanding and dissatisfied, you cite a couple of spots in the dissertation to show how much more work the student has yet to do for the final moment. You yourself may have not spent more than ten minutes to scan the whole body of the student's work. Another issue to note is accountability. Because you are not paid for service, you are not given any negative evaluation if you do not perform your service duty well. For example, you serve on a campuswide board on educational equity. You seldom show up in board meetings. You receive calls from the chair of the board asking for your opinions and judgments on important issues when you are absent from a meeting. Your neglect of service duty is not likely to bring any formal reprimand. The only penalty you possibly face is that you may not be invited for a particular service again. When you develop a general reputation of service dereliction, you may receive fewer and fewer calls for service from people who know you.

Given group hoodwinking behavior and lack of accountability in service, you need to be vigilant, holding yourself to a high standard. On the one hand, you should resist any group attempt to use your name to approve, endorse, or advocate anything you do not fully understand or to which you do not necessarily agree. On the other hand, you should overcome your own temptation to take credit for any service you are not able to perform to the best of your capacity and effort. For example, you should drop your membership on a committee if you are not able to attend most of its meetings and read most of the business materials before each meeting. You should withdraw from a graduate advisory committee if you cannot find enough time to work with the student on various issues pertaining to his or her comprehensive exams, thesis, and job search. You should call the editor-in-chief to take your name off the editorial board if you have not heard from him or her regarding manuscript reviews, editorial policies, and other relevant issues in the past 2 years of your board service. The bottom line is that you conscientiously ensure that you spend an adequate amount of time and perform an adequate amount of labor on a service function even if nobody checks it for you.

Suggestion 5: Serve as a way of life. You may see service as a waste of your valuable research time, a dilution of your rigorous scholarship, or a compromise of your academic integrity. You have cornered yourself in research if you think of service that way. You may then want to adjust yourself to a long-term view of an academic career. There is no doubt that you should concentrate and protect your research at every minute of your scholarly life. It is, however, important that you also take time to mentor newcomers, to socialize with your peers, to maintain the general environment of scholarship, and to test the relevance of knowledge to life in the real world. You do not have to actively seek service. But when service calls upon you, you should selectively respond to it within the constraint of your energy, specialty, and time. In other words, you should approach service as part of your scholarship as well as part of your professional career. For example, you take it for granted that you review manuscripts, evaluate personnel files, and voice opinions on educational policies for your discipline, association, or institution. You ask yourself from time to time: Who else performs those service duties if I do not do my share? How does my research endure and how does general scholarship sustain itself if everyone shuns service? In fact, you can always find room, joy, and benefit for or from service when you take service as a way of your academic life.

CHAPTER 8

TENURE

The majority of academicians gather in colleges and universities. Colleges and universities award tenure to their full-time faculty. Tenure is originally designed to protect academic freedom. It now serves more and more as a means of protection against market dynamics. Faculty members are provided with job security in the mundane world where survival is important so that they can have peace of mind to pursue their somewhat non-secular academic interests. As far as their careers are concerned, tenure may represent a significant turning point for many academicians. One the one hand, it concludes an initial path of success and promise since tenure is awarded on the basis of substantial contributions in teaching, research, and service. On the other hand, it lays a solid foundation for continuous endeavor and excellence because tenure is given with the expectation of a long-term commitment to scholarship through teaching, publication, and service (Alstete, 2000; Baez, 2002; Buller, 2012; Cain, 2012; Chait, 2005; Dobson, 2010; Finkin, 1996; Gray & Drew, 2008; Huer, 1991; Joughin, 1967; Leap, 1995; McCabe & McCabe, 2010; Meiners, 2004; Perlmutter, 2010; Philipsen, 2008; Rockquemore & Laszloffy, 2008; Seldin, 2007; Shoenfeld & Magnan, 2004; Smith, 1973; Tierney & Bensimon, 1996; VanZanten, 2011).

BACKGROUND AND ANALYSIS

There is only one tenure to attempt or possess in an academician's employment career. Many academicians choose not to make mention of

Navigating the Academic Career:
Common Issues and Uncommon Strategies, pp. 57–63

their tenure status in the public presentation of themselves. "Tenured" or "tenure-track" does not seem to appear on the business card, curriculum vitae, or self-introduction by academicians. However, in the back of their minds, academicians working within and outside universities care dearly about tenure. Before they obtain tenure, they fight for it as their ultimate goal. After they have tenure, they use it either as a foundation for an aggressive advance into research activities or as a safe haven from any serious scholarly pursuits. Academic clichés, such as "publication for tenure" and "teaching for tenure," offer testimony that tenure is a focal point and shapes behavior for many academicians in their career-making history.

There have been heated debates over tenure in recent years. Some argue for the elimination of tenure. Others fight for the continuation of tenure. Both sides carry a great deal of emotion in their efforts. Perhaps a systematic analysis of tenure in terms of its pros and cons can only come from a neutral, objective point of view. First of all, what is the benefit of tenure? On the part of academic institutions, tenure secures loyalty, commitment, and dedication from the faculty. It ensures that an institution maintains a stable, consistent, and uniform academic staff in its pursuit of excellence in general and specific scholarly orientations in particular. Universities are the most stable institutions in a market society. Part of university stability may be due to the fact that a university keeps a core faculty through the tenure system. A college may award tenure on the basis of teaching ability. A university that emphasizes research may award tenure only to those faculty members who have achieved certain levels of quality and productivity in scholarship. Tenure therefore becomes a mechanism of selection for the university to keep only those who share its academic mission and goals. Every time tenure is awarded to a candidate, the university awards itself an opportunity for renewal and reinforcement of the spirit of scholarship and excellence it holds.

On the part of individual academicians, tenure means job security and lifetime employment. A job provides income for a working scholar. Jobs offer a stage where career academicians seek self-actualization. Because no other job is more secure than that ensured by tenure, tenure becomes indisputably the most precious gift in the market economy. Tenure proponents also argue that tenure protects academic freedom. Before tenure, a scholar might have to publish articles and books that are politically acceptable in the climate of university, community, and state. Thus a professor who speaks for an unpopular point of view might have to yield to pressures from the political establishment as well as the university administration in fashioning scholarly work, dealing with students, and performing community service. Tenure advocates also argue that tenure ensures quality in scholarship. With tenure, one may be able to ignore external restraints, focus directly on what one is best at doing, and hence turn out the best products one can possibly produce. The underlying assumptions held by tenure supporters are obvious: Academicians are self-motivated, conscientious human beings; they will do best when they are assured of job security and academic freedom; and scholarly quality and productivity will be at the forefront when individual academicians are tenured.

On the other hand, what harmful effects does tenure bring to the knowledge enterprise? From an institutional point of view, tenure prevents a free, healthy flow of academic personnel from place to place across the market or through the community of scholarship. An institution owns a scholar once it grants him or her tenure. An institution may feel that it owns the best scholars possible in the world by its tenure system. But when it fills all its tenured positions, it loses motivation, space, and financial resources to take more creative, imaginative, and productive scholars constantly produced by the market. By owning a core of tenured scholars, an institution may also stagnate, be cut off from new ways of thinking, or be deadlocked into a seemingly active yet essentially useless pursuit. In terms of management, tenure prevents untenured academic staff from meaningfully participating in self-governance and other important decision-making processes in the university. It unjustifiably places power in the hands of tenured faculty. Tenured faculty members are not necessarily more productive and innovative in scholarship. But they are sometimes more vocal, resistant, and rebellious against new policy initiatives. In market conditions, a competitive institution must continuously take in new blood, embrace new challenges, and pursue new programs. With a large army of tenured faculty who navigate in comfort with their favored agenda and their preferred pace of work, an academic institution can soon become irrelevant in the competitive quest for knowledge.

Individually, tenure can make people relax, retreat, and rest. Before tenure, most scholars work hard. They pursue their research agenda rigorously, intensively, and persistently. They treat their students with care, patience, and respect. They respond to service seriously and effectively. After tenure, some academicians slow down and gradually retreat to the comfort of everyday life. In research, they do only what they know or do nothing because they are tired of what they do. In teaching, they may miss classes, muddle through classes, and treat students carelessly as juveniles or hostilely as enemies. In service, they may ignore calls, omit attendance at meetings, and make people wait. Tenure can corrupt people. Before tenure, the majority of scholars consciously and willingly yield to their senior colleagues in both academic and social interactions. They greet them, follow them, sometimes flatter them, and do things big and small to please them. Some may adopt members of the old guard as their protectors. A few may even bribe those in power with monetary, sexual, or social relational favors and benefits. After tenure, some academicians change. They become assertive, aggressive, and explosive, as if they want to regain what they have lost in the past as untenured servants. They begin to exploit social relations, demanding recognition and respect from newcomers. They may start to abuse their position, status, and privileges, enjoying favor and flattery from their untenured colleagues. They may even seek to manipulate academic and administrative processes, imposing their own will, their own version of reality upon those under their control. Tenure politicizes people. Before tenure, most academicians focus on their work. They listen to their leaders, follow rules, and defer to the political establishment. After tenure, some scholars start to diverge from work or research to which they were once committed. They voice concerns, make complaints, and speak out their dissatisfaction. They may openly politick with different factions and enjoy rebelling against management and the institutional establishment. Finally, tenure gives people a false sense of ultimate protection. The majority of scholars are competent, conscientious, and compassionate. They would do well without tenure. In other words, tenure serves for them no positive purpose. Rather, it has made them look weak, incompetent, vulnerable, and hence in need of protection in the eyes of other working professionals as well as the general public. There are hundreds of thousands of scientists and engineers who work in industry, commerce, and government. Embracing market dynamics, many of them spearhead scientific breakthroughs and technological innovations with a rigor no less than that of academicians under the protective roof of tenure. History reveals that protection often leads to individual incompetence and institutional stagnation. Reality demonstrates, again and again, that one does not need protection when one is competent, competitive, and effective in contrast to the market conditions in one's environment.

In all, tenure is a long-established tradition but faces historically challenging conditions. It is a widely followed convention in academia but meets serious doubt, criticism, and noncompliance in new market dynamics. Tenure will not go away soon simply because there are currents running against it. It will not remain the same either, simply because it is deeply rooted in academic establishments and institutional practices.

PRACTICE AND SUGGESTION

Tenure is still in force. Academicians in university settings deal with tenure as a major issue of individual concern. Suggestions are therefore meaningful only if they are made in relation to the existing tenure system

(Alstete, 2000; Baez, 2002; Buller, 2010; Chait, 2005; Dobson, 2010; Gray & Drew, 2008; Hermanowicz, 2012; Huer, 1991; Joughin, 1967; Leap, 1995; Meiners, 2004; Perlmutter, 2010; Philipsen, 2008; Rockquemore & Laszloffy, 2008; Seldin, 2007; Shoenfeld & Magnan, 2004; Tierney & Bensimon, 1996; VanZanten, 2011).

Suggestion 1: Act as if you have tenure when you do not. Tenure is a discriminatory barrier against those who do not have it. In the university setting, tenured faculty members sit on major committees, making critical decisions regarding university policies. Untenured faculty members, in contrast, are evaluated from year to year as probationary employees. They are institutionally denied access to and participation in vital business affairs, such as personnel recruitment and resource allocation, within the university system. While you are not able to change the structural discrimination you face as an untenured faculty, you should stand up against any personal pressure or intimidation from your tenured colleagues. In fact, you should act as if you have tenure in hand. At the department meeting, you do not have to be quiet, receptive, and fearful. You should express yourself, as assertively and fully as your tenured colleagues, when you have a point to make. In research, teaching, and service, you do not have to yield to your senior colleagues. You should do the best you can, no matter how much some of your senior colleagues wish you to be average and regular. Never give up your productivity because some of your tenured colleagues are not productive in scholarship. Never give up your effectiveness in teaching because some of your senior colleagues do not perform in the classroom. Never give up your rigor in service because some of your tenured colleagues advise you on how to dodge service. Your tenured colleagues may make you feel unwelcome, discouraged, disappointed, or even frustrated when you do not follow them in their biased, misleading, or hypocritical advice. But they legally cannot do anything substantive and substantial to harm you and prevent you from advancing in your career if you do well in every aspect of your academic life.

Suggestion 2: Work as if you do not have tenure when you have. Tenure comes with a variety of institutional privileges. Tenured faculty can sit on powerful committees, vote on important issues, and advise department chair and higher level administrators about system policies. With regard to interpersonal dynamics, tenured faculty may mentor their untenured counterparts. Officially, they observe them, evaluate them, and commend or warn them. Unofficially, they may spy on them, gossip about them, and create favorable or unfavorable public opinion surrounding them. Now what do you do when you become a tenured faculty member? Do you follow your hunger for power and influence to exploit, manipulate, or abuse your junior colleagues? Do you indiscriminately respond to all institutional calls to monitor, evaluate, and act upon your untenured counterparts? The answers are obvious. You should focus on yourself, minimize your time in politicking, and work as if you do not have tenure. Specifically, you do not have to offer advice to your junior colleagues if you are not asked for advice and when you do really not have any. You do not have to survey students about how a newcomer is doing in his or her class, even when you sit in a personnel committee. You do not gain any respect from students when you spy on or condescendingly comment about your junior colleagues through or in front of students. On the matter of service, you should activate your sense of professional decency and exert your right to personal dignity. Be resolute and quick to excuse yourself from personnel and other important committees when you yourself are a mediocre performer in scholarship, teaching, and service. Believe or not, you will accomplish a larger amount of work in research, take better care of students inside and outside the classroom, and engage in more meaningful service if you are able to clear yourself from the shadow of tenure, tenure seduction, and tenure protection.

Suggestion 3: Embrace a system of no tenure. Tenure is an illusion. You feel that it protects you. It actually does not. You do not need tenure and tenure protection if you do well. Tenure is not supposed to protect you if you do not do well or if you make serious mistakes. Realizing the nature of tenure, you can free yourself from any false consciousness about tenure. You first drop your resistance to tenure reform or elimination. You then step forward to embrace a system of no tenure. Specifically, you take a long-term, systematic, and progressive approach to career and scholarship. You do not allow tenure to break your whole career into two distinctive phases. You work for the sake of knowledge, not for the purpose of gaining tenure. You measure your success not by whether you obtain tenure, but by the extent to which you fulfill your personal dream. You do not permit tenure to divide yourself into two different persons. You refrain from politicking with your colleagues inside and outside your institution and discipline. You gain respect and influence not by how you manipulate human relations, but by the degree to which you contribute to knowledge.

Suggestion 4: Dream about a system of limited tenure or floating tenure. To embrace a system of no tenure is to overcome the illusion of tenure, to resist the distraction of tenure, and to refrain from politicking after tenure. To dream about a system of limited tenure or floating tenure, where tenure is awarded only to a small number of extraordinary contributors who then have the privilege to carry tenure from institution to institution, is to rise above mediocrity, to excel at scholarship, and to triumph in your career. The system of limited tenure or floating tenure builds more upon a system of no tenure than a system of tenure. It is obvious that limited tenure or floating tenure becomes meaningful and precious only when the majority academicians find tenure out of reach, not when most people can gain access to tenure. In the current tenure system, when you act as if there is no tenure to strive for or to rest with, you may, like everyone else, take 1 day at a time. To distinguish yourself from the rest of the crowd, you need to aim at something that only a few can ever reach in their career. As always, you focus on your work. You do the best you can. You do not satisfy yourself with any temporary or local gains or rewards. You build upon your achievements for ever higher recognitions. With your ceaseless effort at excellence, you will eventually harvest something that only a few may deserve by extraordinary achievement.

Suggestion 5: You do not have to sacrifice yourself to go against tenure. You may be a serious critic, a genuine rebel, or a visionary thinker on the matter of tenure. You can objectively analyze tenure regarding its history, cultural background, institutional foundation, and political ramifications. You can neutrally compare the tenure system to any nontenure option in terms of advantage and disadvantage to knowledge, individual growth, and institutional development. You may ruthlessly expose tenure with respect to its detrimental effects on scholarship, personal character, and organizational practice. You may vehemently push for the elimination of tenure at your institution and through various public forums. But you do not have to be a hunger striker, a sacrifice, or a martyr on behalf of a non-tenure system. If you already have tenure, you do not have to publicly relinquish it to show your determination about tenure reform. If you are about to receive tenure, you do not have to turn it down symbolically to demonstrate your courage for a nontenure system. The reality is that tenure is still in place. When most constituents have tenure, you may not be able to speak about it as legitimately, thoroughly, and convincingly as you could if you yourself were not part of the present system.

PART III

CHAPTER 9

PROFESSIONAL NETWORKING

Employment by a college, a university, or a research institute is a necessary, but not sufficient, condition for one's academic career. To accomplish what is expected of a scholarly life as career, one has to build a personal network for continual research funding and continual publication of research products (Bauer, 1999; Bolman & Gallos, 2011; Brodkey, 1987; Brown-Glaude, 2008; Busch, 1986; Cain, 2012; Clark, Fasching-Varner, & Brimhall-Vargas, 2012; Coser, Kadushin, & Powell, 1982; Darling, 2005; Digiusto, 1994; Fabricant, Miller, & Stark, 2013; Fox, 1985; Kitchin & Fuller, 2005; Lewis, 1997; Locke, Spirduso, & Silverman, 2007; Macfarlane, 2012; McAlpine & Akerlind, 2010; McCabe & McCabe, 2010; McGinty, 1999; Misner, Alexander, & Hilliard, 2009; Powell, 1985; Ries & Leukefeld, 1995; Shaw, 2002c).

BACKGROUND AND ANALYSIS

Network building begins with peers, classmates, colleagues, and former advisors. Although it is often phrased diplomatically as developing common interests, building common ground, and fostering professional congeniality, networking is actually a mode of social adaptation for academic professionals to explore and sometimes exploit human relationships for the benefits of their scholarly careers. Thus, many academicians develop their substantive interests in consideration of funding and publication

Navigating the Academic Career:
Common Issues and Uncommon Strategies, pp. 67–73
Copyright © 2013 by Information Age Publishing
All rights of reproduction in any form reserved.

possibilities. They may even shape and simplify their human contacts toward the "I-Funding-Publishing" triangle that is essential to the realization of their career aspirations.

Funding sources and publication outlets are numerous. Network building around research, finance, and publication takes delicate maneuvering through a complicated social process. For funding sources, there are private and public agencies, national and international organizations, programs oriented toward the practical or the theoretical, as well as various foundations with differing philosophies. While funding decisions are mostly based upon the scientific merit of proposals through peer review, career-making academicians who seek funding for their research cannot afford to underestimate, much less to ignore, the importance of human connections in the whole process. First, researchers need to foster a cooperative relationship with the office of sponsored research at their home institutions. The office may put their names on bulletin boards or add them to information networks so that they can routinely receive announcements and solicitations, electronically or by regular mail, from various funding sources. The office can assist researchers to pass through the human subjects review, develop a research budget, write up sections on institutional support and grant management, assemble proposal components, make copies of the final proposal, and send the complete application to a funding agency. During the execution of a funded project, the office can help researchers maintain routine contacts with the funding agency, manage the budget, and keep schedules for various milestones in the research progress.

Second, academic professionals who depend upon funding from sponsors outside the college or university for their research career need to cultivate a constructive relationship with their main funding sources. For large funding agencies, such as federal grants, they may have to smooth their relationships with a number of departments covering a time period from the receipt of applications, the review of proposals, and the management of project funds to the evaluation of research products. The most important relationship is with the program officer in the funding agency who usually coordinates different components pertaining to funding and funded research. An applicant can certainly benefit from the program officer's insights into the agency's funding priorities as well as the review panel's theoretical orientations and methodological preferences. Preparing an application with those constraints in mind, applicants can greatly improve the chance of being funded for their proposed research. A constructive relationship with the program officer and other stakeholders in the funding agency may even help researchers with special funds and emergency assistance when needed. Psychologically, such a relationship serves researchers as motivation to keep writing proposals and obtaining financial support for their research careers.

Third, academicians who build on funded research in their scholarly careers need to establish peer recognition and support for their research agenda. Funding proposals are reviewed and recommended for funding by a panel of scientific experts. Scientific experts are not heavenly figures. They are peers working in similar areas of specialty. Applicants who have established themselves in an area of research are normally in a better position to receive funding than those who are relatively unknown in the field. Besides scientific reputation, human relations also play a part. Applicants who have made themselves known through a wide net of personal contacts may have a better chance to be reviewed by peers who know them personally. Although it is difficult to verify whether reviewers consciously favor certain applicants, it is possible that they lower their commonsense suspicions regarding an applicant's qualifications to carry out a proposed research or give an applicant the benefit of the doubt in some weak spots identified in the proposal submitted, when they personally know the applicant. It ought to be pointed out that the rule of conflict of interest used by funding agencies in selecting reviewers does not usually prevent personal connections among academic professionals outside their institutional affiliations. It is quite possible that a set group of reviewers used by several major funding agencies in a field cross review each other's grants, lend support to each other's research projects, and therefore perpetuate a research paradigm over a period of time. There might be no detectable coordination on the part of participating individuals. But the situation still qualifies as something approaching a conspiracy that showcases elitism and exclusionary practices in the world of funded research.

With regard to publication, journals, bulletins, magazines, newspapers, and newsletters as well as books, monographs, and edited volumes all serve as outlets for research. Different outlets publish different kinds of academic products, use different selection procedures and standards, circulate to different audiences, and enjoy different reputations in the eyes of academicians. Journals are the best known and most available records of ongoing research within a field. Journals publish research articles, field or laboratory work notes, and book reviews, use in-house editorial or outside peer reviews, cater to scholars in a specific field or discipline, and may be considered by concerned academic practitioners as top, middle, or low-ranking outlets for their scholarly products. Books may report specialized research, propose or elaborate theories, formulate or advocate positions, review major developments in a field or discipline, or present current knowledge for educational and other purposes. They may be printed by commercial publishing houses or university presses for academic professionals, college students, and a more general audience. Publishers may select book manuscripts using judgments by in-house editors or outside reviewers. Books published may receive different ratings depending upon the volume of sales, the number of reviews, and the judgment of reviewers in the academic media. The influence of a journal article or a book is often measured by the frequency of citations by other scholarly sources over a period of time.

While publication correlates mainly with the scientific merit of a scholarly product, some networking by an academic professional with editors, editorial staff, and publishers is also important. It provides the researcher with information, access, opportunity, and encouragement for publishing his or her academic contributions. Information about publications can be general and specific. General information includes what an academic professional knows about all possible publication outlets, their respective aim, content format, submission procedure, review process, readership, and reputation, in the field. It is simply a matter of identifying an appropriate publication outlet once a scholarly product is ready for publication. Time can be wasted if a product is sent to the wrong publication outlet as mere submission and review may take months to complete. Specific information refers to what an academic practitioner knows about a special issue edited by a journal on a specific topic, a monograph series launched by a publisher, and a thematic volume compiled by a fellow academician. These topic-specific issues, series, and volumes may serve as prime outlets for highly specialized products that would be normally rejected by the conventional academic media.

Access and opportunity determine much in a career academician's participation in publication activities controlled by his or her professional associations and employment institution. Journals are sponsored mainly by associations. Publishers usually line up with associations, conference organizers, and institutions on monographs and book series. Academic practitioners who serve on an association's publication committee, an association journal's editorial board, or a manuscript review committee for a publication sponsored by their home institution may be asked to edit a volume by a publisher, take charge of a special issue for a journal, or contribute an article to a book or journal, and therefore have a better chance to publish their own products or to just imprint their name on a publication. For example, in editing a volume of papers presented at a conference, an editor may not only include his or her own products by writing an introduction, some chapters, or a conclusion, but also claim his or her authorship, copyright, and royalty for the whole volume even though most of the articles in the volume were written by individual contributors. To avoid conflict of interest, some journal and series editors may choose to avoid publishing their own products in publications under their editorship. But the fact that they control a publication outlet may still render them better access and opportunity in the whole publication market for selling their own products. For example, editor A may publish editor B's products from his or her controlled publication in exchange for publishing his or her own products through editor B's outlet.

Encouragement is necessary and precious to every academician who strives to actualize himself or herself through publication. Publication, as painstaking it is, can easily lead to frustration, disappointment, and fatigue. From research design to data collection, from data analysis to theoretical exploration, from literature review to the development of an outline, from writing to editing, from submission to review, and from acceptance to publication, each part of the process usually takes months or even years to complete. For example, one may have to wait several months to see the results of peer reviews of one's paper and may have to experience one or two such lengthy reviews until one sees one's paper in print. Given the extraordinary patience and persistence required to deal with the tremendous uncertainty in publication, it is not difficult to see how being approached to write and edit a piece of work with guarantee of publication could change the balance of the game. Indeed, many academicians publish books, book chapters, and journal articles often because of the earnest requests and gentle pressures from colleagues, collaborators, and scholarly friends made at conferences and through associations, projects, employment, and other conscious networking efforts.

Finally, specific relationships with the editor and editorial staff in a journal or publishing house may directly influence the outcome of a manuscript submitted for consideration. The editor makes decisions on whether to accept the manuscript for peer review, to whom to send it for evaluation, and how to interpret the comments by reviewers. In some cases, one may talk to the editor, explaining one's research rationale, suggesting a list of referees to avoid or to include in the review process, and arguing for a new round of reviews if the first round turns out to be negative. The editorial staff receive the manuscript, send it out for review, collect comments from reviewers, edit the manuscript, and prepare the final draft for publication. A smooth relationship with them can bring one multiple benefits. One may easily check the status of the manuscript, expedite the process of review, and give the best possible form to the final product prior to publication.

PRACTICE AND SUGGESTION

Whether you are largely successful or unsuccessful in grant application and publication, you always have something to share with and learn from other scholars as long as you are involved in the process (Bauer, 1999; Bolman & Gallos, 2011; Brada, Stanley, & Bienkowski, 2012; Brown-Glaude, 2008; Busch, 1986; Cain, 2012; Coser, Kadushin, & Powell, 1982; Darling, 2005; Fabricant, Miller, & Stark, 2013; Fox 1985; Kitchin & Fuller, 2005; Locke, Spirduso, & Silverman, 2007; Macfarlane, 2012; McAlpine & Akerlind, 2010; McCabe & McCabe, 2010; McGinty, 1999; Misner, Alexander, & Hilliard, 2009; Porter, 2010; Powell, 1985; Ries & Leukefeld, 1995; Rocco, Hatcher, & Creswell, 2011).

Suggestion 1: Have something to offer before you ask for anything. The world of scholarship is a world of independent, self-sufficient people. Some are more successful, more visible, or more influential than others. But all have their own scholarly egos, ambitions, aspirations, and pride. Scholars judge each other on almost every scholarly encounter, not only on the basis of personal character but also on professional achievement and academic worth. You are on your own as soon as you are out of graduate school. You are supposed to develop and act out of your academic identity when you work and forge relationships with other scholars. You write grant proposals because you have some definite ideas and skills to offer. You submit papers because you have some unique findings and methods to contribute. You join associations because you have some ideas and experiences to share. You will be looked down upon implicitly or explicitly if you cross those bottom lines. For example, you are not likely to receive favorable responses when you submit a rather unorganized and unsubstantiated research paper to one journal after another. You are not likely to become part of or persevere long in any cooperative project if you come with no specific strengths in theorizing, modeling, quantitative analysis, or writing.

Suggestion 2: Never seek a relationship for the sake of relationship. Networking is necessary. Relationship is important. But establishing and maintaining relationships is costly and time-consuming. Be task-oriented, issue-specific, and natural. Let it go when it is over. Do not go to a conference just to initiate a few contacts and make a number of friends. Resist any wishful thinking that by actively seeking advice from a renowned scholar you will be enlightened and encouraged, that by flattering or flirting with some productive folks you will be able to join their projects, or that by helping some fellows with nonsubstantive work in their research you will have your name on their products. Do not ever feel you are important just because you know some famous people, have worked with them, or have conversed with them via cyberspace. Do not ever feel you are part of the crowd just because you know a lot of people in a discipline, having talked to them or having partied with them.

Suggestion 3: Remain open-minded to all inquiries and requests. When you are productive, visible, and influential, you may have to ignore some inquiries and requests from some individuals and organizations. But as a regular scholar, you should always take time to respond to whoever approaches you on academic matters. Be appreciative, prompt, and professional. You may help a student in his or her study. You may lead a junior scholar in his or her early career. You may facilitate grant review and manuscript evaluation. You may serve an organization and community with solid knowledge and sound advice. You may generally contribute to scholarly dynamics as well as social progress. As far as your academic career is concerned, you test knowledge, develop new ideas, gain access to opportunities and resources, forge cooperative relationships, expand research horizons, and enrich academic experiences by embracing various professional activities and obligations in your discipline.

Suggestion 4: Promise only what you are able to deliver. A strong ego and a professionally cultivated motivation for influence and success tend to make many academicians spread a wide net of contacts and commitments to people with whom they themselves often fail to keeping in touch. You need to understand and keep reminding yourself that having some ideas is one thing and putting those ideas into work or writing is another, that thinking of being able to do something is one thing and having done something is another, and that there are always gaps between making a promise and keep a promise. Be honest and courageous enough to say no if you are not able to review a manuscript, render sound judgment on an academic matter, perform a theoretical or statistical analysis, write a chapter, revise an article, finish a book, serve on a committee, or meet a deadline.

Suggestion 5: Keep your promises and deliver whatever you pledge. It is not uncommon that an academic project is delayed, abandoned, or endangered due to one individual's failure to keep a pledge. You may not be disciplined or fined if you are not able to fulfill a promise. But you lose your respect and statue as a trustworthy academic player. People will not return to you for cooperation and participation. You lose valuable contacts and opportunities for service and contributions. It is thus important that you keep promises and deliver your service or products, not only by the time agreed upon, but also in adherence to standards implied or expected. Keep different tasks and obligations in perspective. Set aside sufficient time for each one of them. Never rush through a task in the last minutes. By offering timely and quality services and products to the people and institutions in your scholarly network, you not only solidify your professional relationships, but also sustain general academic processes.

CHAPTER 10

PUBLICATION

Publication is the standard medium by which knowledge is recorded, transmitted, and shared throughout the academic community. To individual scholars, publication provides the basic and oftentimes the only channel through which to participate in scholarly activities and make contributions to the knowledge enterprise. It is difficult to imagine how a career-making academician could become established in a discipline if he or she is not able to develop and maintain a frequent dialogue with the discipline and the larger academic community through publication. If the degree held and the positions assigned are start-off capital, publications are final products in scholarly undertakings, signaling a scholar's substantive involvement in and ultimate worth to the academic enterprise (Barnard, 1990; Becker, 1998; Belcher, 2009; Brodkey, 1987; Buller, 2010; Cain, 2012; Cantor, 1993; Carrigan, 1991; Cox & Cox, 2006; Digiusto, 1994; Flemons, 1998; Fox, 1985; Henson, 2004; Holland & Watson, 2012; Kitchin & Fuller, 2005; Lindholm-Romantschuk, 1998; MacDonald, 1994; Macfarlane, 2012; McAlpine & Akerlind, 2010; McCabe & McCabe, 2010; McGinty, 1999; Parsons, 1989; Porter, 2010; Powell, 1985; Rocco, Hatcher, & Creswell, 2011; Rosenwasser & Stephen, 1997; Shaw, 2002b, 2009; Silverman, 2001).

BACKGROUND AND ANALYSIS

There are different levels of publication in the academic world and beyond. At the outset is the distinction between academic and nonaca-

Navigating the Academic Career:
Common Issues and Uncommon Strategies, pp. 75–80
Copyright © 2013 by Information Age Publishing

demic publications. Nonacademic publications may include commentaries, columns, and feature articles academicians write for newspapers, magazines, and other mass media. They may also include pamphlets, consumer guidebooks, and educational materials that academic professionals write for some practical purposes. They are nonacademic because they do not present any new knowledge, target only a nonacademic audience, and at most involve only the application of academic knowledge to a particular field in life.

Among academic products, a basic distinction is made between refereed and nonrefereed publications. Although the distinction is used conventionally, it actually holds no absolute meaning. First, a manuscript always has to go through some review by the editor or an editorial board before its acceptance for publication. The editor, as the person trusted to control a publication outlet in academia, is likely to be an expert in a specific area. The editor's review of the manuscript serves as a peer review by default. Second, since peer review is stressed as a standard, most publication outlets tend to make claims about their adherence to the peer-review procedure although in fact they may make their decisions by will or by convenience. Third, peer review is a procedure that can be used with a great deal of subjectivity by the editor. On the most possible objective side, an editor may choose reviewers only by the fit he or she sees between a manuscript's substance and a reviewer's demonstrated specialty. On the opposite side, an editor may use potentially friendly or hostile reviewers to accept or reject a manuscript about which he or she has already made a decision in his or her own review. Peer review, in this instance, may thus serve as a rubber stamp for the editor's own judgment.

With all these deviations and variations though, peer review is still the most widely used and recognized quality control procedure in academic production. Peer-reviewed publications, in general, bear a less personal mark from individual editors, editorial boards, or publishers, but have more substantive rigor to catch the attention of a wider academic audience. Major journals in established fields, disciplines, and interdisciplinary domains now adopt peer review as a normal publication procedure. So do most university presses and some serious commercial publishing houses. Products from these sources usually command more attention and respect from concerned scholars.

Among peer-reviewed publications, there are further differentiations in terms of coverage, importance, and influence. A specialty publication, such as journals in medieval religion, drug abuse, and molecular biology, may focus on a specific field and cater to scholars in that field and its related areas. A discipline publication, such as journals in sociology, chemistry, and philosophy, may cover a whole discipline and address all academic practitioners in the discipline. A publication covering a domain of human knowledge, such as a series, breakthroughs, or reviews in natural sciences, social sciences, or the humanities, the three domains of human knowledge, may synthesize knowledge in each domain and attend to the whole community of scholars in that domain. There are even publications that approach issues of interest to academicians of all disciplines and all domains of human knowledge. For each type of publication by topic and audience, there are also different classes or ratings by importance and influence. Discipline journals in sociology, for example, may divide into the prestigious, the important, and the ordinary. An entire group of articles published in ordinary journals may not garner as much influence as does one article appearing in a prestigious journal on the same topic in the same discipline.

Because of the value differentiation in publications, individual career-making academicians tend to frame their publication efforts as well as place their publication products in a hierarchical order. They work on academic publications regularly and respond to nonacademic projects only occasionally or out of special invitations. They use refereed publication outlets mostly and turn to nonrefereed sources only when the latter become the last resort as an outlet to put their ideas and findings in print. They focus on the publication outlets of their specialty but always aspire to reach a wider audience through the more general academic media. They aim high at the prestigious publication media but oftentimes may have to be content with less prestigious and more ordinary choices. Overall, individual academicians take pride if they publish widely in different classes of academic media through different publication outlets. They may also easily develop a sense of failure, inadequacy, and shame if they are not able to publish anything at all.

PRACTICE AND SUGGESTION

Research, writing, and publication take enormous individual talent, effort, and experience. A small thing in individual gift, attitude, network, choice, and lifestyle may make a big difference in research and publication outcome (Belcher, 2009; Buller, 2010; Cantor, 1993; Carrigan, 1991; Cox & Cox, 2006; Digiusto, 1994; Flemons, 1998; Fox, 1985; Henson, 2004; Holland & Watson, 2012; Kitchin & Fuller, 2005; Lindholm-Romantschuk, 1998; MacDonald, 1994; Macfarlane, 2012; McCabe & McCabe, 2010; Parsons, 1989; Porter, 2010; Powell, 1985; Rocco, Hatcher, & Creswell, 2011; Shaw, 2002b, 2009).

Suggestion 1: Research to live and research as a way of life. You are a scholar. You speak the language of scholarship. You see, smell, taste, touch, hear, and think about nature, society, culture, objects, subjects, and the whole world from the perspective of your academic discipline. You raise questions and seek solutions by the spirit of logic, rationality, evidence, analysis, and knowledge. Research is your life. You research for the sake of research. You research as a way of life. You research to live. Depending upon your discipline, you may spend most of your day in the laboratory, in the field, or in the labyrinth of human interaction. You, of course, eat, drink, rest, and sleep. But you always have your mind on research even when you are physically involved in nonresearch activities. As a result, nonresearch engagements may sometimes provide you with inspirations for insights and breakthroughs in research. Programming yourself for a life of research lays a general foundation or sets a basic tone for your scholarly productivity. You create as you grow. You produce as you live day by day. Research, further writing and publication, therefore, automatically become immersed in the constant process of life.

Suggestion 2: Write to build a house and write to record a journey. When you pursue research as a way of life, you turn the writing of scientific design, analysis, and findings into the writing of your reasoning, thinking, and mental activities. You write to record intellectual exercises, explorations, and excursions you make from day to day. You write to express what you want, desire, and long for as an insatiable seeker for truth and knowledge. You write to describe what you attempt, do, and harvest as a tireless explorer of a disciplinary terrain. You write to cap your experience, follow your reflection, and launch your projects one at a time. Writing, therefore, becomes a basic need for expression, organization, and living. You feel uncomfortable if you do not write just as you feel hungry, thirsty, or restless if you do not have food, water, or sex for a certain period of time.

You find the incessant energy of life behind your research and writing when you identify research and writing as your basic needs in life. However, research at each attempt and writing at each undertaking require a structure of careful planning and accumulative effort. You might approach each project as if you were building a house. To build a house, you need to draw an architectural diagram, collect building materials, lay a foundation, and build one piece after another in a logical sequence. Similarly, when you take up a writing project, you need to ask yourself: Do I have a design, do I have all the materials I need, and what time line do I follow? In other words, you write as if you build a house. For each report, article, or monograph, you write one component at a time to complete the final product. In your whole academic career, you write one product at a time to build the ultimate structure of a scholarly identity.

Suggestion 3: Enjoy what you find and appreciate what you write. Acknowledgment is reinforcement. You need to acknowledge what you do in scientific inquiry on a daily basis. You do not wait until you are assured by the scientific community. Specifically, you serve as your own judge when you act as a doer. Every time you do something, you give yourself a definitive judgment: It is good or it is not so good. In scientific exploration, you may find something or you may find nothing. You may follow one thing with another in an orderly manner or you may be misled by the circumstance to nowhere. As the pull to be a sole doer is tremendous, it is critically important that you take time to be a judge at the end of each busy day of doing. You review what you do. You enjoy what you find and experience. Similarly with regard to writing, you read what you write. You appreciate what you write and record. You never discard any piece of your writing even if you are not able to fit it into a larger mosaic of work you are about to present to the scholarly establishment. Instead, you recognize, honor, and celebrate each piece of your writing by typing it out, printing it on paper, and saving it in a safe place.

Suggestion 4: Hear from reviewers to enhance quality and work with editors to improve acceptability. While you perform all necessary rituals to motivate, reinforce, and solidify research and writing as your own idiosyncrasy, habit, and way of life, you know and understand that publication is a social process. You need to use all your communication skills and human relation strategies to deal with the mundane world of reviewers, editors, publishers, and other stakeholders. First is your attitude. You do not view yourself as a scholar with great ideas. You never intuit that everyone in the world needs to hear from you for his or her own good. You do not sanctify your products and further enshrine your ego. You always remember you are one out of a million people who could make the same discovery or come up with the same idea. Specifically, you should charge yourself with being able to explain your research, your findings, and your ideas clearly and effectively. Second is your action. Editors, reviewers, and publishers are human subjects. They expect attention, response, and respect just as you do in social interactions. Editors, reviewers, and publishers are job performers. They work at their jobs and normally attempt to do the best they can. As such, you need to work cooperatively with them, attending to their requests, addressing their queries, making proper corrections, and following their time line. Third is your benefit. As you spend time and energy with all the stakeholders in the process of publication, you will sooner or later find you are in a position to harvest your due benefits. You modify your research, sharpen your analysis, and improve your manuscript upon advice from different perspectives. You expedite the process and put your findings and ideas in the best possible form with aid and encouragement from various players in the world of publication. You spread your work and promote your visibility because of the publication of your contributions in different media.

Suggestion 5: Research, write, and publish as an open process. A geologist may be restrained by his or her mobility when he or she ages. An experimental scientist may not be able to endure the intensity or duration of a scaled project when he or she attains a certain age. However, a scholar should never retreat into nonproductivity as long as he or she is able to think, reason, and live. If you work in a discipline which requires physical strength and endurance, you should continue your research activity even in the last stage of your career by generalizing from empirical evidence, expanding and elaborating theory, developing and modifying technology, critiquing prevailing modes of analysis, or communicating your own experiences to newcomers. If research in your discipline requires only brain, paper, and pen, you can only attempt sublimation and transcendence in scholarship as you accumulate more and more academic observations and reflections in the later years of your life. You should consider the end of your life as the culmination of your scholarship. In all, a genuine scholar does not succumb to circumstance. He or she rises above constraints, physical or mental. The genuine never stops, never retires, and never ends, not for paycheck but only for truth and knowledge. He or she observes, calculates, analyzes, reasons, writes, and publishes, every day and always, to the last breath of his or her life.

CHAPTER 11

GRANT

Scientific research in the postmodern era is seldom an individual pursuit. Research on a single subject often involves investigators in different specialties over a long period of time. Cost for manpower, equipment, space, and operation easily goes beyond the regular budget of an academic institution. In order to carry out their planned research, academicians nowadays need to spend a great deal of time and energy to craft grant proposals seeking monetary support from various private foundations and public funding agencies (Aldridge & Derrington, 2012; Bauer, 1999; Bolek, Bielawski, Niemcryk, Needle, & Baker, 1992; Karsh & Fox, 2009; Locke, Spirduso, & Silverman, 2013; Ries & Leukefeld, 1995; Savage, 2000; Shore & Carfora, 2011; St. John & Parsons, 2004; White, 1983).

BACKGROUND AND ANALYSIS

To individual academicians, a grant is in essence a means toward an end. The means is money. With money, they are able to assemble a research team, purchase equipment and materials, train staff, collect information, analyze data, present findings, write reports, and prepare publications. The end is the research product. It may vary in form, from invention, innovation, discovery, theory, model, methodology, and technical procedure, to a piece of writing in the academic media.

Obtaining a grant is now more and more considered as an achievement in itself. Researchers who obtain grants gain status and importance in the

Navigating the Academic Career:
Common Issues and Uncommon Strategies, pp. 81–86
Copyright © 2013 by Information Age Publishing

eyes of academicians. First, competition runs tight and intense in the quest for a grant. A normal grant application is in most cases a well-crafted scientific piece. It builds upon existing research and some specific pilot studies. It bears the name of its principal investigators and their close associates. In its main body, a grant includes literature review, theoretical arguments, methodological design, proposed research procedures, and expected outcomes on a specific topic. Literature review can be so extensive as to encompass all major contributions to the issue. Theoretical arguments have to be logically derived from prevailing models, paradigms, or explanations on the subject. The methodological design needs to be unique, conceivable, and executable. Proposed steps and actions may be as detailed as they would be in actuality. Outcomes can be imagined and speculated upon. But imagination is always guided by scientific analysis. To emerge from the competition as a winner, a grant as a whole must withstand serious scrutiny and meticulous critiques by experienced experts and scholars.

A grant makes it possible for a group of researchers to work cooperatively on a project, a valuable outcome in any institution of higher learning. It provides the principal investigator with an opportunity to demonstrate leadership in academic research. It promotes the spirit of community among career-making academicians. Most scientific projects are complex, calling for joint work by researchers from different disciplines or institutions. Some projects are multifaceted, creating needs for specialists in different categories, from theorists, logicians, statisticians, historians, computer programmers, methodologists, and experimenters, to writers. Some projects are scaled, generating demands for a number of researchers in similar capacities. Project scholars may work under one roof in a laboratory or at a research center. They may collaborate on a project over distance. But when they work as a team, they develop a collective conscience, group cohesion, and a communal spirit. They motivate one another. They overcome individual weaknesses. They demonstrate team strengths. They benefit from each other in both personal growth and joint projects. Cooperation also gives rise to leadership. On funded projects, principal investigators provide themes, establish agendas, decide on a division of labor, give directions, coordinate individual efforts, and assemble pieces of work into coherent products.

A grant is an indispensable resource in scientific research. It provides funding for manpower, equipment, and other costs involved in research. Scholarship in the contemporary era is no longer an individual endeavor. There might still be a few mathematicians or philosophers who claim that they need only pens and pieces of paper in their favored ivory tower to solve problems, identify formulas, or offer critical insights. Most scientists know they depend upon laboratories, instruments, and other material conditions to gather evidence, analyze data, develop hypotheses, test theories, modify methodologies, and improve models. A scientific laboratory takes millions of dollars to build. A precision instrument or rare reagent may require thousands of dollars to acquire. To obtain one piece of evidence, dozens of experiments may have to be conducted. A whole population may have to be sampled. To develop a feasible model from raw data, network computing may have to be used. To report and spread findings, researchers may deem it necessary to convene a conference for concerned scientists and stakeholders. A monograph may have to be commissioned with a reputable publishing house. All these efforts and activities need time, resources, investment, and commitment. Without funding, much research might never be executed. Without a grant, data might never be analyzed, a presentation might never be made, and publication might never be produced.

Grants are economic capital that empowers academicians in both their academic and secular positions. Academically, well-funded scholars can pursue their research agenda to the extent of their wishes, their wills, and even their dreams. They carry out projects actively, produce reports and publications frequently, participate in disciplinary associations actively, and experience upward mobility quickly. Besides academic visibility and influence, they may assume leadership roles fast and early, inside and outside their home institutions. In their secular aspect, grants enable scholars to make more money than their ordinary colleagues. If they work in universities, they can use grant funds to pay themselves for 12 full months instead of the 9 months for which faculty members are usually paid. They can reimburse themselves for various research-related purchases and expenses. For example, they can change their computer and office equipment more frequently. They can afford to feel less uneasy about the cost of a trip to an international conference. In terms of human relations, grants give scholars more than what they may command with knowledge. With a grant, not only can a scholar advise fellow academicians, but he or she can also hire them and sometime influence them. The power inherent in a grant can obviously translate into control, influence, and a sense of accomplishment for academicians.

Finally, most academic institutions value grant and extramural support as critical indicators of their scholarly activity and institutional vitality. They take measures to accommodate, promote, and reward members who obtain funding from the outside. Indeed, when members bring in grants, an institution receives monetary resources to open programs, upgrade in-house hardware and software, hire employees, enroll students, and boost productivity. For example, a research center is established with federal grants on a university campus. The research center attracts scholars, provides students with research assistantship, and absorbs office staff. It conducts projects, sponsors meetings, and publishes research products. Beyond practical benefits, an institution gains status and stature when many of its members become active, visible, and influential in their respective fields. It may even be given different ratings by reference authorities in education and research in accordance with the total number of grants all its members receive from public and private agencies. A grant brings to the public eye individual scholars. It also makes institutions famous and attractive.

How is obtaining a grant chronicled in an academician's career record of achievements? At the outset, there are numbers of grants in the academician's career pathway. The more grants an academician receives, the more distinguished his or her academic career looks. Grants can be differentiated by their sources as well: private versus public, local versus national, small versus large, and ordinary versus prestigious foundations or funding agencies. Being funded by a prestigious foundation may by itself carry a significant weight in the eyes of academicians. In compatibility with the prevailing view of commercialism in postmodern society, it now becomes more and more a convention that a grant is simply and directly measured by the amount of money received. Each grant is identified too often by its price tag. An academician can boast of funded research throughout his or her entire academic career by dollars in thousands, and sometimes even millions. While a larger amount of money tends to attract bigger attention, it does not necessarily entail more significant contributions to knowledge.

PRACTICE AND SUGGESTION

Before funding providers become serious about any proposal for reform, grants are major resources for scholars in their research career. There are sound ideas and practices to follow in applying, managing, and acting upon grants (Aldridge & Derrington, 2012; Bauer, 1999; Bolek, Bielawski, Niemcryk, Needle, & Baker, 1992; Coley & Scheinberg, 2008; Karsh & Fox, 2009; Li & Marrongelle, 2012; Locke, Spirduso, & Silverman, 2013; Orlich & Shrope, 2012; Ries & Leukefeld, 1995; Savage, 2000; Shore & Carfora, 2011; White, 1983).

Suggestion 1: Work on funded projects with funded scientists. The best way to know the importance of grants and to understand the mechanism of grant-supported research is to work on a funded project with a funded scholar. This can be accomplished first through choice of graduate advisors and thesis. For example, you choose your advisors from among members of the faculty who conduct research with public or private grants. You may ask if you can work on their projects as a research assistant or in a more formal position. You may inquire if you can use their project data for your doctoral dissertation. If you do not find the graduate connection enough, you may consider a postdoctoral fellowship with an externally funded research center for broader and deeper exposure to grant-planning, writing, critiquing, rewriting, applying, submitting, managing, and reporting details and difficulties. As a postdoctoral scholar, you may volunteer or be invited to craft a grant with a team of scientists for a group project. You may take on the position of coprincipal investigator or assume the role of project director. You then have the full opportunity to observe and learn the whole process of grant preparation, application, and execution.

Suggestion 2: Begin with small grants on your own. Even though you have experience with a group of scholars on funded research, you should be cautious and prudent when you apply for a grant all by yourself. You can improve your chance of success if you keep your eye on small grants first. Small grants involve small sums. They support relatively simple projects that do not last long in execution. Grant providers usually do not make stringent demands on investigator qualifications and project outcomes. Most important, there are far more small grants than large ones available for scholars to compete for in the funding market. With a few small grants, some from your home institution, to start off, you build confidence, accumulate experience, expand records, and pave the way for more and larger grants down the stream in your academic career.

Suggestion 3: Build research credentials. No matter how critical a grant is to your research, the moment of excitement you have upon receiving a grant is not the moment of celebration you rejoice in your scholarly endeavor. The amount of money in the grants you receive is not the measure of success you achieve in your academic career. You obtain grants to conduct research. You are ultimately measured by the quality and productivity you demonstrate in research. Even in grant competition, you may initially be betting on your potential to carry out serious scientific projects and to make good on your promises to deliver significant research products. But after one or two start-off grants on your records, you are more and more evaluated by your demonstrated capacities to fulfill grant requirements and your proven records to make important scholarly contributions. You are likely to disappoint yourself, not only in scholarship but also in grant competition, if you do not produce or fail to produce at an adequate level. To build your research credentials, it is essential that you engage in proposed research upon release of grant funding. It is also helpful that you follow some publication standard in each of your funded projects. For example, you may demand of yourself that you turn out at least six publications in prime outlets by the end of a 5-year grant.

Suggestion 4: Become a grant reviewer. Funding providers look for reviewers to evaluate grant proposals from time to time. You should put your name forward for consideration in this service. You may not be paid but you are well taken care of with all your travel costs. There are obviously various benefits from grant review. First, you learn how grant proposals are written and assembled by researchers in your field. Second, you get to know what standards and procedures are put in place by funding providers in grant review. Third, you take the perspective of reviewers regarding important elements of a grant application. Fourth, you forge a close relationship with the stakeholders of a funding agency to which you are likely to submit your own grant applications. Fifth, you make contact with reviewers in your field who may someday evaluate your own grant proposals. In view of all these benefits, you may just want to volunteer to get aboard a grant review panel as long as you are active and visible in research and grant competition in the area of your specialty.

Suggestion 5: Do not become a grant dealer. Writing and obtaining a grant, to some degree, is a craft. The financial benefits and academic control one gains from a successful grant application can motivate one to write one grant proposal after another, without seriously attending to the scholarly responsibilities inherent in each grant. There are even individuals who abandon their academic ambitions and dedicate all their talents and energies to grant hunting in their whole professional career. They use grant money to hire scholars. They make employed scientists work on research projects. They force their name upon the products turned out by hired academicians. They take credit for scholarship just because they have grant money in hand. These individuals are grant dealers. They are shrewd, manipulative, rich, and powerful. They may be featured in the mass media for some of the significant findings made by scientists under their control. But the history of scholarship cannot and will not honor any grant dealer who builds his or her personal fortune and success upon genuine scholars and their scientific contributions.

CHAPTER 12

ACADEMIC AWARD

The distinction between an award and a grant is not always clear-cut in terms of promise and accomplishment. Although it is technically awarded to an academician for what he or she promises to do, a grant for a promised research is in most cases based upon the principal investigator's demonstrated qualifications and achievements. An award is normally given to a scholar for what he or she has done. But it sometimes may be bestowed upon an academician to carry out a yet-to-be-fulfilled activity. For example, one receives a travel award to present one's accepted paper at a conference. In monetary terms as well as in some symbolic indications, the term award may be used interchangeably with grant. A travel award is called a travel grant while a research grant is designated as a research award (Clark, 2006; Editorial Board, 1993; English, 2005; Feldman, 2011; Meyers, 2012; Norbby, 2010; Rhode, 2006; Thelin, 2011; van Fraassen, 2010; Wasserman & McLean, 1978).

BACKGROUND AND ANALYSIS

There are various awards in the world of scholarship. Disciplinary associations sponsor awards for students and scholars within the discipline, field, or area of inquiry in which the awards are established. There may be awards for an excellent student paper, an outstanding publication, a professor of the year, or a distinguished career. Academic organizations make awards for faculty, researchers, and other scholarly staff on their premises.

Navigating the Academic Career:
Common Issues and Uncommon Strategies, pp. 87–92
Copyright © 2013 by Information Age Publishing
All rights of reproduction in any form reserved.

A department may have awards for students in honor of some of its professors. A university may have annual awards for excellence in teaching, creativity, publication, and service. Government is undisputedly the most authoritative player in the delivery of scholarly awards. In a country, the head of state may designate presidential or royal scholars each year. In a province, the governor may from time to time hand out awards to different disciplinary scientists within his or her jurisdiction. Private businesses and foundations are also active in using awards to highlight scientific contributions and celebrate individual achievements in the areas of their concerns and interests. In terms of characteristic features, some awards are prestigious, institutionalized, historical, international, interdisciplinary, publicized, and large in monetary figures while others are less important, local, one-time, specific, less well known, and small in dollar amount. For example, an award for excellence in teaching by a student association may be given to a college professor when the association has a few hundred dollars available in a particular semester. The Nobel Prize, on the other hand, has become the highest honor most scientists in the world ever dream of in their academic career.

An academician obtains awards in different ways: by application, contest, or nomination. Award by application requires that one be willing to file an application, that one submit application documents by the deadline, and that one effectively demonstrate one's deservedness or worthiness for the award through submitted materials. For example, a university provides performance-based merit awards for full-time faculty. Interested faculty members need to document their contributions in teaching, research, and service for varying amounts of awards. A conference-organizing committee offers a number of travel awards for students and junior scholars. Interested attendees are required to include their full papers to be presented to the conference, their curriculum vitae, and letters of recommendation from senior scientists in their applications. Obviously, the key to obtaining an award by application is application. One has no way to obtain the award except through application. One's chance of winning the award is weakened if the application is not strong enough. The reward for a clean and solid application is that one receives the award without any further obligation once the award is made.

Award by contest usually focuses on a specific project, experiment, or activity in scientific inquiry or technological invention. Participants conduct a designated project varying from building a model, solving a problem, inventing a device, developing a theory, and refining a procedure, to writing an essay, on their own initiative, design, and cost. The majority of participants lose while a few win. But the larger the number of candidates who participate in the contest, the higher the quality of the products that emerge from the contest, and the more influence the contest holds in the

circle of scholars. Significant breakthroughs, innovations, and developments may result from a contest. Major publications, even a masterpiece,
may follow after a competition. In history, Jean-Jacques Rousseau made
his debut through a famous essay he wrote for a contest. Award by contest
caters mostly to students and junior scholars. Many academic associations
sponsor paper, speech, and innovation or modification competitions in
the fields or disciplines they represent. Candidates demonstrate their
scholarly potential or special talents by performing a specified task in a
short period of time. They receive an award if they win in a proper category in the competition. For example, when they compete by topic paper
or thematic speech, candidates may be able to publish their winning
paper in the sponsoring association's major journal or make their winning speech to the association's annual convention. In addition, they
receive differential amounts of monetary awards according to their positions as first, second, or third place winners in the contest.

Award by nomination generally applies to distinguished performance
or lifetime service in an institution, a field of study, or a whole discipline.
Academic organizations use award by nomination to promote excellence
and dedication in teaching, research, and service. Nomination may take
place through a formal administrative procedure. For example, each
department is allowed to nominate only one candidate for the college
wide selection while each college is given only one nomination for consideration at the university level. Because only one award is conferred for
overall excellence by the university president, nomination at each level
itself may be regarded as an honor. Disciplinary associations, in a similar
fashion, sponsor an award by nomination to celebrate significant contributions to scholarship. Nominations may be carried out by the membership. For example, all association members are invited to submit their
nominations for the two most influential publications in the past decade
or the two most distinguished physicists, chemists, sociologists, or mathematicians in their time. Individual nominees are first generally recognized for their extraordinary achievements in teaching, research, or
service within their home institution. Or they are well known for their significant contributions to scholarship in their discipline. Only when they
command adequate visibility and a generally favorable reputation, can
they be nominated by other academic participants or their scholarly peers
for an award. Upon nomination, they may be asked to submit proper documentation for formal consideration by an expert panel. The award itself
may be as general as a distinguished career award or as particular as an
outstanding book award.

Most academic awards bring about dual benefits to their recipients.
First is recognition. An award gives an academician a title to identify and
honor him or her. For example, a merit award generates an image of out-

standing performance. A grand winner of a worldwide competition in a discipline carries the pride of achievement and triumph. A distinguished career award gives one's academic life a special distinction. In scholarly as well as secular exchanges, the recipient of such an award commands attention and respect when introduced at a meeting. Second is compensation. Award recipients in most cases receive money or monetary benefits. For example, a well-known scholar may be reimbursed for registration, given a return air ticket and 5-night accommodation at an international conference where he or she receives a book award of one thousand dollars from a disciplinary association. A student who wins an international competition for young scholars in his or her discipline may be paid fully for a weeklong seminar at a world congress. The student may be issued a $1,000 check when he or she is formally honored at the congress. In addition, the department where the student works on his or her doctoral degree may give another thousand dollars as assistance for the trip because of the student's winning the award.

In recording awards received throughout his or her career, an academician may summarize them by totals, dollar amounts, or other quantitative measure. Qualitatively, one may group or divide awards by category, source, or significance. For instance, all travel awards fall in one group. Awards received from within the employment organization are distinctively separated from those received from outside. Awards are ranked by their academic significance. By chronological order, one may simply list all awards in natural occurrence. To combine natural sequence with academic significance, one may chronicle awards from the oldest to the latest while highlighting major ones in bold letters or with special symbols, in one's curriculum vitae.

PRACTICE AND SUGGESTION

Academic awards exist and appear in different phases of your career. Winning an award, losing an award competition, or seeing your peers win one award after another can affect you and your motivation, perception, plan, and commitment. Having a proper attitude toward awards is to some degree necessary and helpful (Doherty, 2008; Editorial Board, 1993; English, 2005; Feldman, 2011; Meyers, 2012; Norbby, 2010; Pratt, 2007; Rhode, 2006; van Fraassen, 2010; Wasserman & McLean, 1978).

Suggestion 1: Be in the loop. As a member of an institution, a discipline, and the world of scholarship, you should know what awards you may apply, compete, or be nominated for, along with the varying roles and statuses you take on in your academic career. When you are a graduate student, you should know various awards for students in your department, college, university, and disciplinary association. Awards from private and public agencies may also be given through university or academic association. As a junior scholar, you may pay primary attention to competitive awards that are designed for newcomers to build confidence, establish a research agenda, and launch a career of scholarly creativity. When you become a senior academician, you may eye mainly the prestigious awards in honor of lifetime achievements or significant contributions. In all different stages, you can make an informed decision as to which awards are best for you to apply for or compete for, providing you know which awards are out there. Even if you do not participate in an award competition, you gain encouragement, inspiration, or spiritual renewal just by witnessing who enters, who wins, and who loses.

Suggestion 2: Take a break for an award competition. You prepare for your comprehensive examinations. You collect data for your dissertation. You rush to your scheduled graduation at the end of a semester. As a student, you may find yourself overwhelmed with all the regular work you have to do for your graduate degree. Amid your heavy study load and responsibilities, however, it is often necessary and beneficial to take a rest for a student competition on or off campus. No matter whether or not you win from the competition, you have the opportunity to revise your paper, reorganize your knowledge, reorient your research, sharpen your skills, make professional contacts, compare yourself to peers in similar situations, and explore the field you are about to enter. Similarly, as an employed scholar, you work on your research projects. You experiment with different modes of teaching. You spend time to serve your institution, profession, and community. You strive for best records in annual reviews. But out of your hectic schedule, you may find it eye-opening and rejuvenating to participate in an award contest for scholars or scholarship in a proper category. By competition, you take a brief break from your scholarly routine. You see new and old forces and trends in your discipline. You compare yourself to others in your field. You feel your own competitive spirit and ability. You obtain validation for your scholarship. The input you gather from a competition may motivate you to take further steps in your career journey.

Suggestion 3: Do not be carried away by one contest after another. While it is beneficial to pause for a competition, it can be detrimental to chase one contest after another in disregard of your regular agenda. There are various awards in the world of scholarship. Each award carries specific benefits, including public attention, money, and human contact. As a student, you may easily be lured into a multitude of contests. In preparation for those contests, you may have to skip your classes, cut short your assignments, and defer your graduation. If you happen to win many of the competitions in which you have participated, you may develop a false consciousness that you can conquer the world by exigently manipulating limited materials to which you have access. You may therefore miss the rightful understanding that you persevere and prevail in scientific inquiry only if you have laid a solid foundation in basic knowledge and skills. As an employed scholar, you are less likely to be seduced by one award competition after another. You are to a large degree bound to your job duty. There are also not a great many substantively meaningful awards for which established scholars can compete. But still, you need to exercise caution and discipline in order not to be carried away by different award opportunities that might exist in your professional environment.

Suggestion 4: Follow your agenda and catch an award in surprise. You may sometimes wonder if you deserve or can someday win a prestigious award in your discipline. But most of the time you just carry out familiar tasks, do what you feel is important and what you can do, without any explicit concern for rewards. That is exactly the right approach you should take toward awards in the world of scholarship. You are a scientist. You engage in scientific inquiry not because you want to win an award. In fact, you are not likely to win an award if you just want to capture the award. An award is not something you aim for. It is something that comes to you when you deserve it. What makes you deserve an award? It is the quantity of your work. It is the quality of your contribution. The logic is then clear and straight. You follow your agenda. You concentrate on your pursuits and endeavors. You receive an award in surprise, just as most Nobel laureates do.

Suggestion 5: Use an award to compensate yourself. The impact of awards on scholarship is more general than specific. Most award sponsors do not expect the specific recipients of their awards to make another extraordinary contribution for winning another of their awards. They mainly intend to inspire and motivate the general target audience to excel in the subject their awards are designed to promote. If you receive an award, you should first compensate yourself for what you paid, lost, suffered, or endured in winning the award. Pay off your debts. Take a vacation. Improve your living conditions. Raise the quality of your life. After all those compensations, you then plan to invest in your research for a yet higher level of productivity and contribution.

CHAPTER 13

MEMBERSHIP IN ACADEMIC ASSOCIATIONS

Most academic associations are now open to people who apply and pay membership dues. Qualifications or achievements are no longer seriously questioned in the membership application. On the part of career-making academicians, however, membership in academic associations still gives them a sense of identity, belonging, and professional pride. It provides them a forum to communicate research, a network to gather feedback, and a community of nurturing for continuous academic pursuits. In fact, all essential elements of academic life, including presentation, service, and publication, are basically realized within the purview of academic associations (Cion, Frey, Sorskin, & Sevick, 2012; Coerver & Byers, 2011; Cox, 2007; Dalton & Dignam, 2007; Dewsbury, 1996; Haskell, 2000; Jacobs & Assante, 2008; Peck & Stroud, 2012; Professional Convention Management Association, 2006; Sachs, 1990; Sladek, 2011; Weddle, 2007; Young, 1985).

BACKGROUND AND ANALYSIS

Academic associations are formed by members of various disciplines in the knowledge enterprise for their specific scholarly pursuits. But once they are established, they possess power to represent and influence individual academicians in a discipline or a field of study.

Navigating the Academic Career:
Common Issues and Uncommon Strategies, pp. 93–99

On the matter of representation, an academic association can serve as advocate, spokesperson, negotiator, and protector for the members of a profession or an area of inquiry. As advocate, it justifies the necessity of a knowledge branch in economic production and argues for social support in the form of funding and an adequate number of personnel. For instance, an association of chemical engineering may put out advertisements about the critical importance chemical engineers play in the production of consumer goods, urging young people to join the profession in their search for lifetime careers. As spokesperson, an academic association issues statements about its mission, its professional goals, and its policy positions on current events. An association for Middle East studies may condemn violence and propose peace as an alternative solution to conflict. It may back up its positions with research done within the sphere of scholarship it represents. As negotiator, an academic association may engage in explicit or implicit interactions with its neighboring disciplines over territorial claims. For instance, an association of anthropologists may claim its exclusive right to the study of an ethnic culture in a remote island whereas an association of sociologists maintains that its members are best equipped to study the island society. Negotiation may lead to cooperation and sharing of learning between the two disciplines. As protector, an academic association defends its members against cultural critique, political scrutiny, and institutional evaluation in their scholarly pursuits and career movements. For example, an association of teaching scholars may provide testimony about the academic value of pedagogical research when one of its members experiences trouble in his or her tenure or promotion review with publications on teaching and student learning. An academic association may also take part in political processes to secure benefits and safeguard rights for scholars and practitioners under its umbrella.

The effectiveness of representation by an academic association lies in the characteristics of its members. The number of members it includes under its organizational roof is important. The more members it represents, the more bargaining power it has in negotiation with other parts of society. The nature of the work in which members of an association engage is highly relevant. The more indispensable the work done by its members is to a society, the more importance an association may claim for itself in social interactions. Thus an association of medical scientists may exert more influence than an association of sociologists. The association of medical scientists may have to defer to an association of nuclear engineers in power at a time when the country is strategically committed to building an atomic bomb. The level of productivity of its members is also relevant. The more productive its members are in research, teaching, and service, the more visible an association is in a discipline and in the larger society. An association of criminal justice scholars may attract more attention than an association of social workers if members of the criminal justice association are more productive in their scholarly work. Political activism is from time to time critical. The more active some of its members are in political arenas, the more limelight an association may enjoy in social presentation. An association of political scientists may make the media, the government, corporate interests, or the populace take notice of it, not so much for the serious academic work its members do, but rather because of the numerous public demonstrations some of its members organize in confrontation with the political and economic establishments. Finally, some academic associations may apply the trick of "association" to communicate to the general public or boost their standing in the larger society. They may use celebrities in politics, the media, entertainment, or the business world to suggest that the discipline it represents can inspire one to become a successful person or that the profession it promotes can lead one to an illustrious career. For example, an association of psychologists may refer to some well-known persons in government, even though the latter just hold degrees in psychology or have long abandoned their practice in psychology.

An academic association can shape its members and their career-making efforts by various institutional means through which it communicates with its members. By the publication outlets it controls, an association can explicitly or implicitly push members into peculiar research paradigms or agendas. At one time, it may favor theory over application, quantitative research over qualitative study, or one area over other areas of inquiry. At another time, some sections or theoretical, methodological orientations may gain popularity under its auspices. By the presentation forums it runs, an academic association obviously determines what theme members follow in its annual convention, what issues they debate, and what topics, theories, and methods they may have to highlight or ignore in regional and sectional meetings. By the service opportunities it affords, an association may tax the reading capacity and the willingness to serve of a few old hands or political insiders with academic reviews, legislative testimonies, media interviews, convention organization, and association maintenance. Meanwhile the majority of its members are left out of the loop. An academic association usually sponsors competitions, confers honors, and delivers awards. By singling out specific members and membership deeds for recognition, it influences the minds of its members as to what is important and valuable in a field of study. An academic association also creates among its members a general sentiment about their discipline, profession, competency, effectiveness, and social status. Whereas an association of scholars in the study of government may often feel uplifted by what they explore, an association of drug abuse researchers can sometimes feel tainted by the subject matter they study in their professional career.

The influence an association can have over its members depends upon its members and membership characteristics. In a discipline or a field of study, not all scholars or practitioners join the association that exists for them. Among those who do pay membership dues, not all of them present their research to the annual meeting, publish their products in association journals, cast ballots for association officers, and offer news for the association newsletter. A large number of association members are simply observers. They pay attention to what goes on in the association for their specific area of inquiry. They participate in substantive activities only when they are seriously interested. The number of products turned out by association publication outlets in a discipline depends on who control those publication outlets as editors, editorial board members, and reviewers. While an association may sponsor a flagship journal or monograph series in a field of study it represents, it does not have control over where people in the field publish. In fact, when association journals are dominated by a small group of members in one extreme theoretical or methodological orientation, the majority of the membership may come to regard these journals as remote sources of reference or outlets for publication. The people who become association leaders are individual members. They are elected into association leadership not always because of their widely acclaimed contributions; from time to time, people take office because of connection, ideology, and luck. When an association is controlled by a group of advocates who are viewed as extremists, that association may not necessarily represent the mainstream concerns and interests of the membership. Finally, the sheer size of the membership of an association may say it all: How seriously it is taken, whether it provides primary publications, and whether it represents prevailing interests and sentiments by or for scholars in a discipline or an area of inquiry. An association may possess only an empty name of representation if a large number of scholars it claims to represent do not belong to it and if it does not hold the hearts of most active and productive people in the discipline.

Although they are voluntary and have obvious limits in representation and influence, academic associations overall can shape academicians and their research interests over a career or life span. Out of ordinary associations, there are elite organizations. They offer membership as an honor to those who have demonstrated extraordinary worth to the knowledge enterprise. For instance, national academies of science, engineering, or medicine in many countries award their membership only for exceptional contributions. Membership in those exclusive organizations not only generates a pride of accomplishment and influence for a few outstanding performers, but also provides a source of inspiration and encouragement for many ordinary doers in their academic careers.

PRACTICE AND SUGGESTION

There are hundreds of academic associations of interest to you in your scholarly career. Some are close. Others are remote. Some are academically driven. Others are politically charged. Some are helpful to your academic interests. Others are of no use for your scholarly pursuits. You may choose to stay away from most of them. But you still need to deal with some of them for information, exchange, and opportunity. A general attitude or strategy is therefore in order (Coerver & Byers, 2011; Dalton & Dignam, 2007; Dewsbury, 1996; Haskell, 2000; Jacobs & Assante, 2008; Peck & Stroud, 2012; Sachs, 1990; Sladek, 2011; Weddle, 2007; Young, 1985).

Suggestion 1: Pay close attention to all related associations. Your area of inquiry sits in a particular location in the whole hierarchy of the knowledge enterprise. It is likely to fall under a large discipline. It may include subdivisions. It is likely to relate to similar areas of inquiry or fields of study within and without the large discipline to which it belongs. Academic associations are usually formed to cover not only the larger discipline, but also division, subdivision, and their intersections within the discipline. By paying close attention to all the associations related to your area of specialty, you have the opportunity to scout the most challenging issues for research, the closest fellows for collaboration, the most facilitative media for exchange, the most understanding audiences for presentation, the most relevant areas for service, and the most appropriate outlets for publication. You obtain perspective on what you do, how important it is, whether it attracts a crowd of competitors, and what future it offers. You may also gain advantage in research refocusing, job change, and career movement. Because you know who your neighbors are and what they do, you can easily identify and relocate to a more suitable subdivision should you become burned out in your existing area.

Suggestion 2: Attend one of its annual meetings before joining an association. The best way to learn about an association is to attend one of its annual conventions. At the meeting, you can make general observations as to who its members are, how they relate to each other, and how they conduct association affairs. You can scan conference programs, sit in sessions, and read papers or abstracts to develop a sense of what its members do in research and whether they are active, innovative, and productive in their individual academic pursuits. You can reinforce your impression about association members and their scholarly activities or contributions by collecting flyers, viewing books on display, and examining sample journals at registration desks, information booths, and book exhibitions. You may also talk to other conference participants, both members and non-members, about their sentiments toward the association. By one whole conference experience with an association, you may already be able to make an informed decision as to whether to join or stay away from it.

Suggestion 3: Stick to one or two most relevant and helpful associations. Commitment works. Loyalty pays. Dedication moves. After a period of open exploration, you should focus on one or two associations you feel are most relevant and helpful to your scholarly pursuits. They may be regional, national, or international. They may be specific to a subject, a discipline, or an interdisciplinary field of study. You pay your dues. You volunteer for service. You attend their annual, seasonal, sectional, or regional meetings. You read their newsletters. You visit their websites from time to time. You subscribe to their journals and read articles pertaining to your specialty. When you are ready, you organize sessions for association conferences. You submit your manuscripts to association journals. Gradually, as you become reputably recognized, you may occasionally or regularly receive opportunities to serve as an association officer, an award reviewer or judge, a manuscript or grant evaluator, an editorial board member, or even an editor. Consistent membership also qualifies you for special honors and highest leadership roles should you become so established and deserving through scholarship. On a personal level, persistent involvement may give you lifetime friendship with people in your field.

Suggestion 4: Serve your way up. Be humble. Be courteous. Be of service. Like employment organizations, an academic association provides you with institutional means and opportunities for scholarly growth and career mobility. But before expecting and receiving anything from your committed academic association, you should first ask yourself what you can offer to it. In a broad sense, you should concentrate on your area of specialty and make the best contributions you can to knowledge. You enhance the status of your association, discipline, and profession when you, as a member, participant, or practitioner, turn out quality products to benefit people in the larger society. Specific to service, you should begin with labor-intensive work before you assume any role of power and influence. For example, you attend registration desks, sit behind information booths, set up conference rooms, hand out flyers, maintain websites, and take notes when you are a student and junior member. A few years later, you organize conference sessions, serve as session chair and discussant, review manuscripts, and assume leadership roles in association chapters or sections. After another few years, you sit on editorial boards, edit association newsletters, serve as association secretary or treasurer, and make preparation for an even higher level of involvement in association affairs. When you are academically established, you may then run for editorship of major association journals, association vice-presidency, and association presidency. Those positions may afford you power to leave some of your personal marks on your association, discipline, profession, and even the knowledge enterprise. But to get there, you need to pave the way for yourself through a whole sequence of serious service and extraordinary contributions.

Suggestion 5: Focus on academic activities. You may have different expectations for your participation in an academic association. Socialize and have fun. Make serious friends. Visit different places while attending its annual meetings. Seek service and volunteer opportunities. Develop and keep a feel for the field or discipline. While you can embrace all these possible benefits, you should align each of them with your scholarly pursuits. You socialize with other scholars in similar specialties because you may be inspired by some of their thoughtful remarks, enlightened by some of their insightful comments, or just reminded about some critical issues or lines of analysis by some of their casual talks. You make serious friends because friendship leads to mutual encouragement, motivation, and collaboration in scholarship. You visit different places because you want to develop a global view of your academic field, regarding who does what, how, and where. If you work in a field within the humanities or social sciences, you may broaden your understanding of human conditions from place to place. You seek service because you may enhance your research through service. You obtain a feel for your field or discipline not because you want to cheer or lament what everyone else does in the discipline, but rather because you need to build upon what is available and make the best possible contributions to the field. The key is to remember what you are trained for and what you are supposed to do as a trained, socialized, and disciplined scholar.

CHAPTER 14

CONFERENCE PRESENTATION AND PARTICIPATION

Presentation is confined to a particular time and occasion. Its influence is usually limited to the audience who are present at the presentation. Also, because of the spontaneity of the information transmitted and various setting or time-specific constraints inherent in oral expression, presentation is not as detailed, accurate, and long-lasting as publication in the communication of academic materials. On the other hand, presentation is quick, simple, and direct in spreading new ideas and findings. More and more conference organizers invite academic and nonacademic media to their meetings and publish conference abstracts or proceedings for larger circulation. Presentation can therefore become an effective means to report, publicize, and share most recent developments across an academic discipline (Berkun, 2010; Cion, Frey, Sorskin, & Sevick, 2012; Coerver & Byers, 2011; Cohen, 1997; Dalton & Dignam, 2007; Fenton, Bryman, Deacon, & Birmingham, 1997; Hyland, 2006; Jacobs & Assante, 2008; Peck & Stroud, 2012; Professional Convention Management Association, 2006; Reinhart, 2002; Rendle-Short, 2006; Reynolds, 2012; Shaw, 2001b; Sladek, 2011; Weissman, 2011).

BACKGROUND AND ANALYSIS

In the individual profile of an academician, presentation may serve as a barometer of the level of activity in which he or she engages in his or her

Navigating the Academic Career:
Common Issues and Uncommon Strategies, pp. 101–108
Copyright © 2013 by Information Age Publishing
All rights of reproduction in any form reserved.

academic career. It may also provide a measure of visibility and influence in an academic field. Presentations can be tallied and compared by number. An academician who has made fifty presentations to academic gatherings may legitimately feel that he or she has better access to the academic world and higher visibility within it than someone who has made only five presentations. In quality, presentations may divide into different categories, forms, or levels by different standards. For instance, a presentation may be identified by the conference in which it was made: local, national, and international or field-specific, disciplinewide, and interdisciplinary conferences. It may be classified by the form in which it is made: informal roundtable, formal roundtable, poster, oral, or thematic. There are also differences in whether a presentation is invited or unsolicited, made to a small group panel or a thematic plenary session, and regarded as a regular or keynote speech. An academician who has made numerous unsolicited general presentations to various academic conferences may offer no comparison, in academic visibility and influence, to one who has made only a few invited keynote speeches at the annual conferences in one's discipline. As a rule of thumb, keynote speech and feature presentation to a plenary session at a major academic conference are reserved for only a few outstanding contributors who have established their positions in a discipline through publication.

To the general relationship an academician has with a discipline, presentations fulfill a number of major functions. First, the presentation takes one to a conference, a gathering of academic participants in a field or discipline. At the conference, one appears as a whole person, not just a name as one does in a piece of publication. One dresses in style or casually. One speaks with or without an accent. One listens carefully or with no regard to details. One smiles wholeheartedly or superficially. One makes gestures now and then, conveying one's intent and feelings in a sophisticated way. One asks questions thoughtfully and responds to queries quickly or pointedly. All these physical acts and features converge to create a public image of an academician. One may therefore make oneself known to be a person to befriend, a person to seek advice from, a person to collaborate with, or a person to distance from by other participants in the field or discipline with which one is associated.

One's presentation also can introduce what one is doing or about to do in research. Compared to publication, a presentation can be introductory rather than conclusive, preliminary rather than final, incomplete rather than complete, and informal rather than formal. An academician can use a presentation to make a public announcement or statement about what he or she is pursuing or intends to pursue in an area of inquiry. Interests and expectations may then be generated. Collaborators, partners, or competitors may be identified. Advice, critiques, and suggestions may be gathered. Publication outlets, communication channels, and possible audiences may be explored. With regard to a potential research paper, specifically, one may be able to collect useful comments from the audience so that one can substantively expand or deepen literature review, data analysis, theoretical discussion, or policy application in the main body of the paper. One may receive an invitation, by phone or in writing, from an editor so that one can contentedly and confidently prepare one's presented paper for publication consideration in a journal or in a monograph series.

Third, oral presentation supplements what one is able to convey through publication. Presentation is complementary to publication in a variety of ways. It highlights what will be or is in print. Reading a research monograph may take days. Perusing a scholarly article calls for hours of serious attention. Through presentation, however, an author may use the interactive setting to summarize main points or convey underlying assumptions in his or her work in a few minutes. With major highlights in mind, readers can easily walk through the whole text and gain a command of its content in detail. A presentation explains what is written on paper. In a scholarly piece, there are always descriptions, arguments, illustrations, formulas, figures, or reasoning that are not immediately clear and understandable to readers. The author may have to resort to oral presentation to address queries and offer proper explanations. Thus oral presentation serves as a prelude to what is forthcoming in publication. An author may take a book tour in which an oral presentation arouses interest in the author's forthcoming work. Speaking to an academic conference, the author may simply direct the audience to one of his or her scheduled publications by saying "Please read my book, when it is out, if you would like to learn more about what I have said in my presentation today." Oral presentation offers closure to what remains on written record. After reading a piece of work, readers may be informed, convinced, and inspired or lost, unconvinced, and squelched. An author and his or her advocates may have to engage in public presentations to build on what the author has written and to transmit their conviction of its rightness to the audience. Also, there are people who take and retain information better when it comes in the form of oral presentation rather than in the form of writing. Even when they know and understand some ideas and reasoning well in written language, people are more likely to internalize and follow those ideas and reasoning in their own research and analysis when they receive reinforcement by hearing directly from the author.

Fourth, oral presentation highlights what one has done in scholarship. Publication is often scattered in pieces through different outlets. Although individual pieces add up in a scholar's rise to prominence, each piece itself may not give its author a particularly intense feeling of success, pride, and glory. Oral presentation, on the other hand, can be made to a large audience in a magnificent setting where the presenter can spectacularly highlight his or her position, status, and influence in a field or discipline. In academic gatherings, one may be invited to make an opening or concluding speech to a plenary session. One may be offered the opportunity to deliver a keynote presentation at a lunch or dinner banquet. One may be given the opportunity to offer a thematic exposition of one's contributions or career while receiving an award. As the sitting president of an academic association, one may even be entitled to provide a presidential address, conveying one's vision for an entire field or discipline. All these formal presentations are designed for presenters not only to communicate their achievements, contributions, thoughts, and visions, but also to receive cheers, recognition, honor, and admiration.

Finally, oral presentation celebrates the spirit of community in academic undertaking. Academicians, by training, are abstract, analytical, and logical specialists. They read articles, calculate numbers, make logical inferences, write books, and build models. They communicate with one another, mostly and essentially, through publication. From a purely utilitarian point of view, academicians do not have to spend time, energy, and resources on trips to academic conferences. They can just sit in front of computers, stay in libraries or laboratories, and cruise through electronic and published media, to achieve success in their academic endeavors. By birth, however, academicians are ordinary human beings with flesh and blood. They eat food, drink water, and engage in sex. They need interaction. They desire companionship. Each year, hundreds of thousands of academicians attend meetings and conventions in their field or discipline, for the most part, because they want to be acquainted with each other, to know and be known, to impress and be impressed, to please and be pleased. At the meetings, they shake hands, exchange words and nonverbal cues, give and receive greetings, give and hear presentations. They chat, walk, dance, laugh, eat, drink, and entertain, one on one, in groups, or jointly at large. The ultimate effect of all those activities is manifest and symbolic: to renew human ties and to keep a sense of community among fellow academic participants.

PRACTICE AND SUGGESTION

Presentation is part of academic communication and interaction. But an approach to conference and presentation may run from one extreme to another. On the one hand, you may jot down some ideas on a piece of paper, take a flight to the conference destination, rush to your session, talk about your ideas to a few absentminded strangers in the audience, and then spend the bulk of your time on sightseeing tours surrounding the venue. On the other hand, you write a complete paper. You prepare slides, transparencies, or power-point presentations. You fly into the city a couple of days early so that you can adjust to the locale; you sit in on different sessions to feel the spirit of the conference. You make your presentation to an active, knowledgeable, yet respectful audience. By the time the conference is concluded, you feel so positive about it that you do not even want to leave.

There are indeed good and bad conferences, serious and cynical conference goers, conscientious and careless speakers. Whether a conference becomes a fleeting experience or a genuine learning experience, to some degree, depends upon your own attitude toward presentation in general and the conference in particular. As a career academician who influences and is influenced by the spirit of academic community, you may want to consider the following suggestions on the positive side (Berkun, 2010; Cohen 1997; Dalton & Dignam, 2007; Fenton, Bryman, Deacon, & Birmingham, 1997; Jacobs & Assante, 2008; Peck & Stroud, 2012; Reinhart, 2002; Rendle-Short, 2006; Reynolds, 2012; Shaw, 2001b; Sladek, 2011; Weissman, 2011).

Suggestion 1: Present only when you have a complete paper. You are eager to be on a conference program, sharing your ideas and findings with other practitioners. You are anxious to meet with people in your field or discipline, developing a sense of who they are, what they do, what they value, or even what they look like. You cannot wait to take a break from what you do on a daily basis, joining in the fun with people of similar training and interests in an exotic land. No matter what motive you have in your mind, you need to make sure you have something substantive to offer in your presentation and to the conference. The yardstick is a complete paper, a simple indication of your full preparedness for meaningful participation in a formal academic occasion. With a complete paper, you have sufficient amounts of materials for selection and inclusion in your presentation. When you receive further interest from the audience, you have something definite to hand out at or after the conference. Most important, a conference becomes beneficial and successful only when you are serious about it and everyone else concerned is as conscientious and responsible as you in attitude and behavior.

Suggestion 2: Use visual aids. Presentation involves both verbal and nonverbal cues and clues. The audience receives information not only by sound, but also by sign. Between sound and sign, signs composed of colors, graphs, diagrams, and drawings can be more attention-catching and mind-striking. Another important factor is the conference itself. People attend the conference with a mode of reception different from what they use every day in their office or laboratory. They are normally on the verbal, abstract, and analytical side when they read books, peruse articles, and hear lectures in their academic institution. They tend to shift their mode of reception from the abstract to the concrete, from the analytical to the sensual, and from the verbal to the nonverbal when they go to a conference where they expect to be interactive. Still another factor is the condition of your own body and mind away from home. At a conference, you may suffer from jet lag. You may lose sleep. You may be nervous. You may exhaust yourself with excessive levels of activities. With information neatly contained in slides, transparencies, and power-point presentations, you can be worry-free about how you have to adjust yourself for different highs and lows in your presentation. You can just follow your visual aids through the whole process. In other words, visual aids can be your best safeguards for an optimum performance in the conference situation.

Suggestion 3: Sit in on sessions with interest and questions. You know you have to read serious materials to obtain essential information in your field. But you are at the conference. It does not hurt to attend different sessions to hear general ideas and current developments in different areas of inquiry. Information you receive at the conference may be sketchy, superficial, and fleeting. But it can be thought-provoking, inspiring, suggestive, and mind-opening. After all, you understand that what you hear in a session is just an introduction. If you are interested in a piece of information, you need to take further steps to obtain the details or to verify its validity and reliability. Sitting in on a session, you should be free from any assumption, bias, expectation, and judgment. Be attentive, respectful, and receptive. Listen carefully. Take notes. Ask questions. Make comments. Give suggestions. But do not question the speakers about their qualification, intent, ideology, theoretical orientation, and methodological preference. Most important, do not overtake the speakers to make your own statements about an issue. Remember you cannot possibly gain anything by attempting to show off in someone else's show. Beyond individual integrity, you make an impact by acting appropriately at the conference. In the final analysis, the conference depends upon individual participants in all its aspects. If you and everyone else attend as many sessions as possible and behave as professionally as you possibly can at each occasion, the conference will surely become a positive learning experience for all.

Suggestion 4: Attend business meetings for service opportunities. Academic associations operate by volunteerism and participatory democracy.

Formulation of vision, creation of agendas, and allocation of resources are not necessarily done by people who have distinguished themselves through academic contributions. In fact, critical decisions are often made by people who are willing to show up in business meetings. Important actions are often carried out by people who happen to land in a position and are willing to follow up on their assigned responsibilities. Associations hold most of their business meetings on the site of annual conventions. If you are interested in academic service, you should make an effort to attend some of your national or regional association's business meetings. You may initially feel cynical about how important issues can be decided by a seemingly small group of not necessarily the brightest and the most scholarly people in your association. But when you sit down and become involved in the meeting's process, you may gradually understand why things go one way or the other. You then begin to feel comfortable to raise your hand or not to raise your hand on issues of which you know little and do not understand thoroughly. You volunteer to sit on a committee or to serve as a session organizer, a newsletter editor, a sectional meeting convener, or an association secretary. It is important that you begin with heavy-duty service and proceed cautiously to power-holding position. It is also important that you keep your service role and expectation in perspective with what you hold in your home institution. You are likely to disappoint yourself when you are a 1-year old assistant professor attempting the presidency of your subdisciplinary or regional association.

Suggestion 5: Greet strangers to expand academic contacts. Attending a large academic conference can be either a socializing or alienating experience. You go to different sessions, hoping to make some meaningful contacts. But no one seems to be interested in engaging in any substantive conversation before, during, or after the session. People run around and rush away by saying "Excuse me, I am late for a meeting" or "I am sorry I have a session to go to in just one minute." You walk in the hotel lobby and conference hallways, seeing people chat in pairs or have fun in groups. You wonder why you are alone, having no one to talk to or no group to join in. You wander in the city street, seeing people wear the same type of name tag or carry the same type of bag as you from the conference. You feel you want to greet them. But they stride, chin up, as if they do not care to know who you are. You seem unimportant to them. On the surface, everyone comes for the meeting but no one seems to be really interested in meeting with each other, especially with you.

In the final analysis, however, you need to realize that you are an average participant. You are like everyone else at the conference. If you feel lonely, a lot of other participants may feel lonely, too. If you feel you want to talk to someone but lack sufficient courage or just do not bother to break the silence, many other participants may feel they are in the same situation. If you leave one encounter for another because you feel you may miss an even more important occasion, a majority of other participants may do just the same with exactly the same mindset. At any large gathering, people tend to operate in a fleeting state. They do not focus on things. They chase things. People tend to wrap themselves in specific facades. They may pose as persons of definite views even though they walk aimlessly from one session to another. They may act as if they are sociable, popular, or important even though they are lonely, fearful, and desperate to make new connections. Recognizing the essence of human behavior in public gatherings, you can turn your convention experiences into socializing and networking opportunities. Overcome your own ego, fear, and indolence. Be honest, down to earth, and active. Greet strangers. Embrace acquaintances. Be the first to ask questions, extend hands, and break the silence. Cherish each encounter. Invest in each situation. By working on one contact at a time, you may forge some meaningful relationships at the conclusion of each meeting you attend.

PART IV

CHAPTER 15

ACADEMIC CAREER PATHWAYS

An academic career pathway refers to the general career process that academic professionals in a society or historical era move through in their lifelong scholarly pursuits. It is specific to a society because scholars may follow different career paths in different social environments. It is specific to a historical era because academicians may take different career routes due to different historical forces. A typical career pathway in a particular society or era, however, is not necessarily universal for all academic practitioners therein. Obviously, some academicians may deviate from the general pathway by passing through its stages in different sequences or by dropping off in the beginning or the middle of the journey (Azzarello & Ferrazzi, 2012; Blaxter, Hughes, & Tight, 1998; Brown & Brooks, 1996; Feldman, 2013; Gardner & Barefoot, 2010; Garfinkle, 2011; Gould, 1978; Grant & Sherrington, 2006; Heinz & Marshall, 2003; Hermanowicz, 2002, 2012; Levinson, 1978; Miedaner, 2010; Piper, 1992; Rajagopal & Lin, 1996; Tierney, 1997).

BACKGROUND AND ANALYSIS

In the context of modern and postmodern society, an academic career pathway generally consists of five stages: initiation, routinization, secularization, solidification, and graduation. Each stage involves specific tasks. It invokes peculiar false assumptions as well. At the stage of initiation,

Navigating the Academic Career:
Common Issues and Uncommon Strategies, pp. 111–122
Copyright © 2013 by Information Age Publishing
All rights of reproduction in any form reserved.

prospective academicians tackle five major tasks. The first is attaining proficiency and competency. Prospective academicians attend graduate school, learn the academic language, and command essential skills. The second task is learning norms and normative behavior. Prospective academicians follow requirements, familiarize themselves with customs, and internalize basic rules. The third task concerns identification and identity. Here, novices meet insiders, learn to identify and respect giants, and follow role models in the field. The fourth task concerns specialization and specialty. Academicians build motivation, develop interests, and decide on a focused area of inquiry. The last task involves adventure and experimentation. The academician conducts research, becomes familiar with presentation and publication, and moves through the larger professional waters in various academic media.

The false assumptions that academic beginners often make typically fall under five categories. First, "I can conquer the world." One is obsessed with grand ideas and ignores technical details. One is overjoyed by acquaintance with monumental achievement in scholarship but underestimates the meticulous effort involved in developing a masterpiece. One focuses on substance but fails to see the emotional sentiment involved in academic undertakings. Some representative acts are these: One openly criticizes a professor for misinterpreting a theory in class; one sends a manuscript to an editor in attempt to overthrow a dominant paradigm. Second, "I am not fully responsible." One succumbs to the weak side of oneself. One is reluctant to put the whole of one's learning or the truth of one's position into scholarly presentation and publication. One condones one's own mistakes. A typical reasoning is: "I am a student, not a professor. It is no big deal if I misunderstand something, engage in unprofessional practice, or mess up a situation." Third, "It's still too early for me to try." One is fearful. One is self-inhibited. One defers written examinations, postpones final defenses, and bypasses opportunities for professional presentation and publication. For example, when some professors ask one to contribute a chapter to a volume they are editing, one turns it down by saying "I have not taken any course in that area yet. I am afraid I have to focus on my coursework now." Fourth, "I am not ready yet to enter the profession." One idealizes the romance of student life within the walls of the university while dramatizing the brutality of survival in the academic market. One registers for classes one after another and participates in aimless discussion in classroom settings. One is addicted to an entertaining yet unproductive type of intellectual exercise among university faculty and students and thus never graduates. A proof of the phenomenon is this: It takes more and more PhD candidates longer and longer time to complete their training. Lastly, "I don't think I can make it there." One admires influential figures. One fears one's own mentors. One mystifies disciplinary theories and methods, overestimates the talent and effort required for quality work and significant achievements, and is blindly in awe of academic establishments. An illustration is: "I am an ordinary person. I don't think I am born to dream for those big things. I will be happy if I can just manage to survive with all these talented people."

Routinization is the stage when one settles into a tenure-track position in an institution. One of the major tasks one has to deal with is to get to know the job, the institution, the profession, and the disciplinary establishment. Specifically, one needs to learn rules, familiarize oneself with existing conventions, empathize with prevailing sentiments, and establish a network of interaction, reference, and support. Second is to build a teaching portfolio. One has to identify a set of courses one is good at teaching, prepare syllabi and course materials for each of those courses, set ground rules for conducting class, interacting with students, grading, and handling complaints, and cultivate a teaching style characteristic of one's own fluency and comfort. Third is to develop a research agenda. To start off, one needs to retreat from those grand ideas one embraces during graduate school or overcome those characteristic feelings of unpreparedness and unsureness one goes through as a student. One then must take the initiative to identify one's own strengths and weaknesses, delve into an area of specialty, program oneself into a research way of life, and place oneself, properly yet uniquely, in the whole knowledge enterprise. Fourth is to open and maintain a track of service. One needs to make oneself known and available for service related to one's expertise. Depending upon one's needs, interests, and visibility, one may actively seek opportunities for service or turn down various requests for service. Regardless of personal situation, service is necessary and important in keeping oneself in balance between personal success and social responsibility in the phase of routinization. Fifth is to put the academic career in proper perspective with various commitments in life. Settling into a community, one naturally asks: Should I get married if I am single? Should I raise children if I am married? Should I purchase a home if I have a family? Should I develop some new interests in life? Or should I invest savings in bonds, mutual funds, or stocks? All these questions require thought and effort to answer. Along with academic concerns, these personal issues shape and reshape one's career in general and routinization in particular.

An academician becoming routinized should stay alert to the five common false assumptions many of his or her peers tend to make at this stage. One assumption is this: "My advisors and classmates are out there to support me." One keeps calling on one's graduate advisors, asks them not only for advice, but also for substantive assistance. One talks to former classmates about one's sufferings, and may even weep in front of them. One who acts in this fashion may unfairly drag someone in one's graduate training into one's routinization process. Another false assumption is "I saw that or I did that in graduate school, differently from what you guys do here." One tells one's students and colleagues, in classrooms and in department meetings, what one saw or did in graduate school, and implies what they do now and here is awkward, backward, or outright wrong. One who makes such comparisons may unnecessarily offend the old guard in one's college or university. Still another common assumption is "This is not what I expected." One struggles between the ideal and reality. One feels that one's students are underprepared and ill mannered. One laments that one's colleagues are coldblooded and hostile. One resents that one's leaders are repressive and evil-minded. One complains or looks for an exit from one's situation. One who so reacts is likely to change jobs frequently. The fourth assumption is "I cannot do research because I am preoccupied with teaching and service." One is fearful of research. One spends time in the laboratory but never turns out anything. One collects data but never analyzes them. One juggles a lot of ideas but never puts anything on paper. One may do every little thing in teaching or service to avoid research. One may even lie to oneself: "I will get back to research as soon as I gain an upper hand on teaching and service." One who so excuses oneself may find it more difficult to pursue research in the later phase of one's career. The fifth common assumption is "I have to put a lot of things in life on hold so that I can get my career under control." One isolates oneself in one's office. One calls around, attends meetings, and chats with students and colleagues. One plays with words, numbers, and models. One follows most of one's activities and days in academic settings. When approached for life-related issues, one habitually responds with the simple answer "I have no time for those luxuries." One who so programs oneself may never find time for joy and happiness in life.

Secularization begins when one is tenured and becomes immersed in one's institutional as well as disciplinary establishments. At this stage, an academician identifies with prevailing norms and conventions, by practicing them, teaching them to one's students, and defending them when they are breached. In teaching, one rests with one's own methods, style, and reputation. One may be known for teaching a set of content courses and being casual, permissive, discursive, and boring or demanding, organized, inspiring, and helpful to students. With colleagues, one complainingly or jokingly talks about students being unprepared, uncooperative, disrespectful, or not as good as they used to be some time ago. Sitting on committees regarding students, one may argue for or against tough educational standards. One may torture or spoil an advisee with reasonable or unreasonable assignments. On the matter of research, one digs year after year in an area, by similar theoretical and methodological approaches, and with similar findings and publications. One reviews manuscripts in the area. One sits on editorial boards or rises to the association leadership in one's discipline. One is at ease with one's specialty, enjoys a certain level of visibility, and feels one is part of the knowledge enterprise. In service, one responds to calls for advice and expert opinion from the community, the government, and the media. One may take the initiative to organize a conference, run an association, edit a journal or book series, or engage in other academic undertakings. One makes money, gains respect, and extends influence. Finally, secularization makes one settled into a peculiar work routine and lifestyle. One may be known by janitors, security guards, secretaries, or neighbors for leaving the laboratory late every day, guzzling several cups of coffee after lunch, or taking walks in the neighborhood before midnight. Most important, one relates to people in other occupations in a way that typifies one's calling in academe. For instance, one may sound like a scholar even when talking about news and movies with next-door neighbors. Life activities and routines characteristic of academic efforts do not exist merely as side products. They serve as powerful reinforcements in scholarly endeavors. Developing a lifestyle compatible to academic endeavor, therefore, can be considered as one of the main tasks a secularizing academician works on in a scholarly career.

The most common false assumption held by a secularized academician is: "I know it all." One teaches classes off the top of one's head. One pages through new publications without serious reading. One writes papers following a set track of thought. One shakes one's head when seeing things out of the ordinary. To newcomers, one tends to assume "I am an insider." Under this assumption, one pours out stories, experiences, and versions of reality to the newer arrivals. One joins old colleagues to monitor, gossip about, manipulate, or even "torture" the newcomers. One labels them "naive," "inexperienced," or "unrealistic" when the newer arrivals experiment with something new or something one simply dislikes. One loses sight of the fact that these newcomers are the force of the future and the hope of one's institution. To students, one assumes the stance, "I am always right." With this assumption, one lectures students, orders them to conduct different exercises, or even forces them to attempt something out of their reach. One calls students "lazybones" or "uncarveable wood" if they do not live up to expectations. One fails to realize that one can be wrong and may learn from students. To people in other walks of life, one may be quick to assume "I am more educated, informed, and rational than all of you." With this assumption, one looks down upon common citizens as being ignorant and gullible. One criticizes politicians as being wicked and manipulative. One laments the media as being biased and misleading. One is too presumptuous to appreciate the vividness of the larger social mosaic. The last common false assumption a secular academician is likely to make regards future and change: "I am not going to be different." One brags about one's years of service. One takes comfort in what one has accomplished in teaching, research, and service. One sticks to accustomed ways of thinking and acting. One resists change, innovation, and reform. One refuses to back down even in confronting mistakes made.

Solidification does not necessarily follow the stage of secularization for all career-making individuals. It builds upon or emerges from secularization among a small number of academicians. Sitting in full professorships, a great many faculty on university campuses feel they have arrived at their career destination. At most, they keep doing what they are familiar with doing, becoming ever more secular along their career pathway. A few, however, attempt to rise above their secular experiences. They reach the uncommon stage of solidification when they are successful. There are three paths toward solidification. One is through scholarly accomplishments. One makes extraordinary discoveries, puts forth revolutionary theories, develops unusual methods, produces masterpieces, or spearheads a new area of inquiry. One becomes the president of one's disciplinary association or is awarded highest honors in his or her discipline, such as the Nobel Prize. Another is by way of management. One is fortunate to be pushed, often through political maneuvering, into the chairmanship of one's department. The experience as chair makes one eligible to apply for a managerial position at the dean's level. The experience as dean sets a stage for a further ascendance to leadership at the university level. In one's second track of management after the first track of scholarship, one sharpens public speaking skills, strategizes human relations at different levels and in different settings, manipulates resources and opportunities, plays fundraising tactics, and relates properly to the larger political environment surrounding his or her job duty. As one becomes a career administrator, one gradually loses the drive and instinct for serious academic contributions. Still another route toward solidification is through establishing a practice or service. One capitalizes on one's training, knowledge, or invention. One establishes a business or opens a practice. As a business owner, one may become more and more concerned with profit and eventually abandon one's aspiration for scholarly breakthroughs. Or as a practitioner, one may gather firsthand data from clients and develop a theory or a treatment of scientific importance. No matter what route one takes in one's academic career, one needs to make a significant effort to emerge from the mundane, the secular, or the transient to become solidified in the unusual, the exceptional, and the eternal.

A career academician who reaches the stage of solidification can also make and act under false assumptions. The two general assumptions shared by many solidified scholars are: "I am special" and "I represent it all." By the first assumption, one feels one is a genius, blessed with the special talent, skill, or opportunity to discover what others are not able to find, write about what others fail to see, control what others are incapable of handling, or profit from what others are unaware of. With the second assumption, one feels one is the sovereign of one's discipline, institution, or profession. One may declare that one's discipline is in a theoretical or methodological crisis, calling for a general reform or revolution. One may proclaim that one's institution must commit to a particular philosophy or standard, forcing all its members into a set track of thought or a fixed mode of behavior. Specific to different routes of solidification, one is likely to assume that "knowledge is power" if one gains influence through scholarship. As one is admired and honored for one's widely used theory or method, one may intuit that it is possible to conquer the whole world just by knowledge. Similarly, one is likely to assume that "power is everything" when one sits at the helm of an academic institution. And one is likely to assume that "money speaks" if one runs a knowledge-based corporation. In the first scenario, one sets rules, gives orders, and applies rewards and penalties. One sees clearly how one can manipulate the mass of secular academicians, even the stars of scholarship, by the power one holds. In the second scenario, one keeps a development team of scientists and engineers within one's company. One hires, fires, promotes, or demotes those scientists and engineers. One feels one can easily manipulate them, no matter how much knowledge they have, as long as one has money to employ them.

The last stage is graduation. Although some academicians vow that they will never graduate from scientific inquiry, others admit that they cannot wait to retreat back to the wishes of their childhood, the excitement of their hobby, or the comfort of their family life. As far as employment and job duty are concerned, graduation is indeed an inevitable and important phase of a complete academic career. The major tasks one is faced with at the stage of graduation include these: reviewing, winding up, repositioning, adjusting, and slowing down. Review involves both a retrospective examination of past work and an objective evaluation of current projects. In examining work throughout one's career, one sees ups and downs, gains and losses, pride and regret. The question is: Can one build upon one's achievements to move further or can one make up any of one's losses? By evaluating one's ongoing projects, one can responsibly decide what to terminate, what to hand over, what to leave behind, and what to carry on. Winding up is based upon review. Using the time left on active duty, one wraps up an experiment, an analysis, or a manuscript. Most important, one may be able to clear a critical hurdle in the effort to establish a theory or method, unravel a puzzle or problem one has long dreamed of solving, or conclude a capstone project one has been pursuing for years. Repositioning is to evaluate oneself and identify a proper niche for oneself during retirement in the knowledge enterprise. Depending upon one's experience, reputation, network, energy level, and time commitment, one may deliver guest lectures from place to place, take short-term residency with a research center, participate in an issue-specific project, engage in writing, or volunteer in a service or educational organization. Adjustment is needed as any new line of activity in retirement requires a different approach, expectation, or perspective than one is used to through the preretirement career. There is a time of ease and joy when one acts upon a wealth of lifelong learning. There is a time of frustration and sadness when one is confronted with challenges previously unheard of. Finally, slowing down is to admit the declining mental and physical power available for academic activities one is able to engage in as one draws close to the end of life. One keeps an eye on the academic world, reads scholarly articles, and may occasionally come up with some critical ideas. But overall, one knows that one is on the back stage of the knowledge enterprise, moving closer and closer to the absolute conclusion of one's academic career.

In a mood of graduation, a career academician can easily make false assumptions, specifically about his or her contribution, career, and discipline, and generally about life and science. Beginning with one's contributions, one may assume: "Nobody really understands what I put forth in my theory or method." With a feeling of betrayal, one may criticize the disciplinary establishment and admonish the mass of scholars for their inattention, obtuseness, and carelessness. Regarding one's career, one may feel: "I have nothing to be proud of." With a feeling of lack of self-worth in scholarship, one avoids talking about one's past work or the institution where one was employed, shows no motive to explore academic markets for research and teaching opportunities during retirement, and takes joy only in nonacademic hobbies or volunteering activities. With respect to one's discipline, one is likely to assume: "It's no longer my world." One has some ideas about one's discipline but buries them in one's mind, feeling that nobody would care to know about those ideas. On the matter of life, one may assume: "No life ever exists beyond my academic career." Under this assumption, one refuses to retire from academic work but continues a long habituated daily routine, with or without scholarly productivity. One retreats to life only when challenged by a disabling disease or other drastic event. Finally, a graduating academician may cap his or her scholarly career with some general thoughts about science and the knowledge enterprise. One may assume: "Science is a game," and complacently aligns oneself with the large army of smart players in academia. One may assume: "Science is the world of geniuses," and sentimentally characterizes oneself, along with the vast mass of ordinary academicians, as simple materials used by, or as little dwarfs in the service of, a few pioneers and leaders in the production of knowledge and domination.

PRACTICE AND SUGGESTION

There are always pride and regret, satisfaction and dissatisfaction, as well as reinforcement and modification over career pathways. Through the process, focus is put on performance, efficiency, effectiveness, and productivity. In the end, reflection is often transcendental about the consummation of academic career and the quality of mundane life (Azzarello & Ferrazzi, 2012; Blaxter, Hughes, & Tight, 1998; Feldman, 2013; Finkelstein, 1984; Garfinkle, 2011; Gould, 1978; Hermanowicz, 2012; Levinson, 1978; Maslow, 1954; Miedaner, 2010; Piper, 1992; Rajagopal & Lin, 1996).

Suggestion 1: Live a simple life. Life is a multidimensional sponge. It can easily absorb all your time and energy. As a scholar, however, you do not have to avoid or abandon life. You can live and enjoy every essential element of life while pursuing your academic career. The key is to streamline your life, free yourself from unnecessary life engagements, and, live simply. For example, between single and married life, you may choose a married life but you should select a spouse who understands your passion for knowledge and achievement, and therefore does not so often pressure you to join him or her in a daylong trip to the fishing pond or the shopping mall. Between having no children and raising children, you may choose to have children, but you should not expect to enjoy a large family of children. Between renting an apartment and purchasing a house, you may choose to own a house but you should not stretch your budget and your time to maintain a huge estate with an extensive collection of furniture, arts, cultural relics, pets, plants, flowers, and other decorative items. Between saving money and making an investment, you may choose to invest in the market but you should not attempt to chase stocks or mutual funds for best possible yields. Between work and hobbies, you may choose to follow a hobby but you should be aware that you cannot afford to embrace it with an addictive level of enthusiasm. There are big and small choices in life. Living a simple life often means that you choose a thing or a way of doing things in its basic form, without spending more than necessary time, money, and energy on it.

Suggestion 2: Enhance your work with your life. Depending upon your discipline, you may benefit enormously from your life observations, reflections, and experiences as fertile soil or motivation for serious philosophical contemplation, theoretical generalization, historical description, and policy analysis. Fighting as a soldier in Vietnam could not only motivate you to become a specialist in Vietnam, but also provide you a real-world perspective in your analysis of the country. Dealing with various moral dilemmas in life could make you a more thoughtful scholar of ethics. Being married and having children could offer you critical insights and motivation to delve deeply into the issues of marriage, family, childhood, adolescence, and personality development. Regardless of your discipline, you can always develop a reciprocal relationship between work and life. For example, you are deadlocked in your search for a concept, a formula, or a line of reasoning. You are suddenly enlightened while walking with your spouse under the moonlight, playing with your kids in the yard, or chatting with your family members at the dinner table. You are disappointed, frustrated, or tired with your work. You are gently refreshed, recharged, and rejuvenated with courage, insight, and energy after a visit to your hometown or a vacation with your family. Overall, life is what you begin and end. It is in living you find the real meaning of success. Only a life of peace, love, and family support can bring work and scholarship into harmony.

Suggestion 3: Enrich your life with your work. Divisions of scholarship loosely correspond to areas of life. You may strike the best possible deals on home purchase and financing if you specialize in real estate and home mortgages. You may maximize your financial gains from stocks, mutual funds, bonds, and other savings plans if you concentrate on investment, insurance, and banking in your areas of scholarship. You may favorably influence your family diets, health habits, and lifestyles if you study medicine, public health, or nursing. You may take an informed, balanced, or holistic view of life, society, and history if you major in a discipline in the humanities and social sciences. In general, you are educated and habituated to emphasize evidence, logical analysis, and rationality in exploring nature and to apply imagination, empathy, and sympathy in studying human dynamics. You may use your education and career experience to help you deal with real life issues. For instance, you remain calm and clearheaded when others become emotionally upset in a time of fear, terror, and other crises. You seek truth from facts or can take the perspective of others when you are drawn into conflict with neighbors, relatives, or a stranger in the shopping mall. You quickly simplify and rebuild your life when you encounter economic, political, or emotional difficulties.

Suggestion 4: Be the turtle, not the rabbit. You are familiar with the folk story about the race between a turtle and a rabbit. The turtle moves slowly but he keeps going in his journey and ultimately wins the race. The rabbit starts off with a huge lead but opts for a nap in the middle of the competition and eventually ends up as a loser in the game. You may think you are brilliant. But your best bet for success is to be as humble and persistent as the turtle. Be alert all the time. Be content with a little progress each day in your work. Feel bad or even guilty if you take your mind off your work for a considerable period of time. Feel frustrated if you do not finish a task in a reasonable time frame. The inner pressure you have on yourself provides you with basic forces for devotion and dedication. The constant attention you pay to your subject puts you on track toward important findings and major breakthroughs. On the other hand, a honeymoon, vacations, arguments with your spouse, failing grades on the part of your children, a broken-down car, unavailable references, and various daily hassles in life and at work can easily balloon into big excuses for disruption from work. You may never find a complete chunk of time for your academic work if you look for a perfect time when you can wholly concentrate on what you want to do. There is no perfect time nor ideal situation. You may solve a mathematical problem, discover a chemical reaction mechanism, or develop a sociological analysis procedure when you play with your children in the park, lie down on the hospital bed, or wait in the supermarket line for some daily purchase. The key is to put your mind on your scholarly pursuit and make use of every bit of usable time for it in your life.

Suggestion 5: Respect the convention but do not be conventional. The world, the academic world in particular, is well set up. You need to follow rules and conventions to be recognized and accepted by the academic community. For example, there is a standard language for papers. There are established formats for presentations, styles for references, and codes for conduct. It is not wise to irritate insiders with a form or an appearance that is completely alien to them. An unusual form may alienate members of the old guard to the extent that they will not accept even conventional content from you. On the other hand, if you package your ideas well in conventional form, you can often sell unconventional substance to an academic audience. Here then comes the first half of a general guideline for you in your academic career: Respect conventions. Defer to seniors. Listen when they talk. Do not speak out unless you have something important to say. Read instructions for authors before you submit your manuscript to a journal. Make all necessary changes when you receive comments from reviewers and the editor. Bring copies of your paper when you present it to a conference. Observe the time limit. Use an overhead projector and other props. Speak clearly on your major points. Answer questions patiently. By following the conventions, you save time, facilitate the process, and make yourself part of the system. But who am I? The question brings up the second half of the suggestion: Do not be conventional in substance. Always ask yourself: What can I offer to my area of inquiry, my discipline, or the knowledge enterprise in general? Embrace innovative ideas, methods, and ways of analysis. Strive for new findings and breakthroughs. Think differently and do differently with regard to subject matter on a day-to-day basis. In the end, you make a successful career only when you contribute. You contribute only when you come up with something new, different, or perhaps even unique. You turn out something new, different, or unique only when you are unconventional in your way of thinking and acting throughout the whole journey of your academic career.

CHAPTER 16

SCHOLARLY IDENTITY

What makes a scholar? What accomplishments or residues lie within an academic career? What image does a career-making academician attempt to build for himself or herself in his or her institution, discipline, society, and era? The curriculum vitae seemingly provide a condensed display, a crystallized reflection of an academician's career sequence and structure. Within the vitae, education and degrees usually appear in the forefront, indicating an academic aspirant's origin and background. Following this information are the jobs and positions held at employment organizations, signaling an academic participant's secular status and power. Publications, teaching, presentations, professional activities, and community service constitute the main body, representing an academic practitioner's substantive activities and contributions to the knowledge enterprise. Honors and awards cap the vitae at its conclusion, summarizing a career scholar's visibility, reputation, and influence in the world of scholarship. It is taken for granted in the academic circle that the best way to know a scholar is not to talk with that person or to read his or her papers, but to review the person's curriculum vitae.

In general, the degree, position, publication, teaching, presentation, service, grant, award, association membership, and tenure are key elements in an academic career. Each element is important in its own right and takes a significant part, if not the whole, of a career-making process to develop, grow, and substantiate. In the meantime, these elements relate to each other in importance to form the structure of a career or a chronicle of achievements that builds an academician's self-identity and

Navigating the Academic Career:
Common Issues and Uncommon Strategies, pp. 123–129
Copyright © 2013 by Information Age Publishing

shapes future attitudes and behavior in his or her continuous career-making endeavor. For instance, publication by itself is a record to build for a lifetime. It relates to all other career components or in the mind of many scholars serves as a leading force to organize other aspects in the whole structure of academic life. A publication-centered career structure, once formed or in the process of formation, obviously affects how a scholar defines priorities, pursues research, engages in scholarly and nonscholarly activities, and maintains a public image throughout his or her career-making journey (Abdelal, Herrera, Johnston, & McDermott, 2009; Caughey, 2006; Cownie, 2004; Di Leo, 2003; Engvall, 2003; Garber, 2001; Graham, Emery, & Hall, 2012; Halvorsen & Nyhagen, 2011; Piper, 1992; Stinchcombe, 1999, 2000; Talburt, 2000; Tomlinson, 2013; Whitchurch & Gordon, 2010).

BACKGROUND AND ANALYSIS

Making an academic career involves developing a scholarly identity. In building one's scholarly identity, one meets specific requirements and fulfills general achievement standards in major categories, from education, institutional employment, teaching, and research, to service. For instance, research involves publications, grants, projects, and presentations. Teaching includes courses taught, pedagogical innovations, the number of students served, and the ways in which students will say they have been changed by the instructor's teaching. Although it presents only one aspect of a scholarly career, a particular category of scholarship may dominate the whole identity of an academician. In other words, a scholar can become so strong in one area of scholarship that accomplishments in that one area say everything about that person's scholarly identity.

The whole-part contrast relates directly to the compartmentalized versus multifaceted orientation in the construction of a scholarly identity. Under a multifaceted orientation, a scholar strives to cover every base of his or her academic career. One has a doctoral degree and feels one has fulfilled the licensing requirement for academic practice. One works in an academic institution, with proper access to scholarly stimulation, resources, and opportunities. In teaching, one constantly explores new ways of instruction and proves to be a dynamic and inspiring professor inside and outside the classroom. On the matter of research, one writes proposals, conducts funded projects, presents findings to professional audiences, and publishes articles and monographs through academic media. Besides teaching and research, one actively engages in service, from organizing conferences, editing journals, reviewing manuscripts, and serving on committees, to advocating for policy changes, within and outside one's institution, community, and discipline.

Under a compartmentalized orientation, however, a scholar delves into one area and is not able to do much work in other areas. For instance, one has been teaching a fixed set of courses in a community college since receiving the doctoral degree. One seldom presents work to professional conferences and has never published anything in academic outlets. One goes home after teaching and is barely in the service of the discipline, institution, and community. Although claiming to be a teaching scholar, one does not have much to offer regarding pedagogy and general crafts-manship of instruction. In other scenarios, some scholars claim to be pure researchers. They are fully devoted to their own research, leaving little time for instruction and service. They miss class, go to class unprepared, or run class without clear objectives and agenda. Students cry for help to little avail. They never answer calls for service, hardly even show up in committee meetings, or keep only a nominal appearance on service occa-sions. There are also scholars who claim to be advocates, reformers, or service professionals. They engage in social movements, community activ-ism, or expert testimonials in the media, the court, or the legislature. They do not offer much academic substance in classroom instruction nor have they published any considerable amount of serious, theoretically sound and empirically grounded, work in their discipline. They basically use their doctoral degree as a selling point for some of their personal and social ideologies.

Another important contrast in the building of a scholarly identity is individual expectation versus institutional demand. Individuals may choose teaching, research, or comprehensive universities. They may opt for governmental agencies or private industries. As far as academic aspi-rations are concerned, one may want to be a devoted instructor, an accomplished researcher, or a social activist. Personal aspirations are obvi-ously moderated or constrained by individual perceptions, abilities, and resources. One who is fearful of research may find face-to-face interaction with students a justifiable escape from the usually lonely academic inquiry. One who cannot sit down long enough for serious reasoning and writing may feel one can only channel one's knowledge and training through ser-vice and social advocacy.

In the meantime, institutions where individuals work exist as powerful sources to shape and reshape individuals in their career design and devel-opment. A liberal arts college may only want its faculty to make students and their parents happy. It may not care much whether a faculty member publishes in academic media. A research-intensive institution may pres-sure its faculty to publish in leading academic outlets. It may turn a blind eye to how a faculty member performs in classroom and whether numbers of students complain about him or her. A comprehensive university may expect its faculty to do a little something in all three areas: teaching, research, and service. In the end, it may only gather a collection of scholars who do not stand out in any one of the three areas. Industries and governments are known to restrict their employees from freely saying and writing about issues related to their work and specialties. They want their academically trained employees only to apply state-of-the-art theories, methods, or technologies to solve specific problems within their functional operation. As more and more individuals follow market forces to enter institutions outside their choice, institutional demands seem to become more and more imposing and dominating to override individual expectations in the development of a scholarly career and identity.

Still another important contrast is idealized versus actualized identity. The contrast applies to both individuals and institutions. At the individual level, there are people who aim high and work hard but are not able to achieve even half of what they dream for. Although they remain unfulfilled, they still credit their high dreams and ideals to what they have actually attained. They believe they would not have reached where they are had they not been motivated by their lofty goals. On the other hand, there are people who are surprisingly successful even though they never give much thought to how high they want to reach in their academic career. They harvest their first gain by luck, under some patronage, or through hard work. They then seem to roll on to success with all forces coming to their aid.

At the institutional level, universities and research organizations put out faculty manuals, codes of conduct, or employee handbooks, specifying official requirements for tenure, promotion, or special awards. Strictly by written requirements, an institution should only garner a collection of geniuses, first-rate scholars, all-rounded high achievers, master teachers, or social engineers. In reality, however, gaps always exist between words and deeds. While an elite institution may house primarily high-achievers, in all likelihood, it will harbor some mediocrities as well. While a metropolitan university may dominantly draw classroom teachers, it may also include a few poor instructors as well as some productive scholars in its ranks. In a sense, written words from the employee guidebook are more about how an institution wants to be perceived by its employees and the general public than about reality. Once a public perception is formed about an institution, individuals often voluntarily choose to join or leave the institution. The institution, therefore, significantly spares itself the likely confrontational enforcement of personnel rules and regulations. For example, individuals would not apply for employment in a highly competitive university if they knew their career ideals did not measure up to the performance standards of the university. They would leave the university before the year of critical decision if they knew they would not survive or if they could not feel some sense of comfort, control, and dignity in the university of which they want to become a part.

PRACTICE AND SUGGESTION

No one is certain what he or she will ultimately emerge to be. Identity is in the making, at every moment and from moment to moment. Intentionality may take the lead in identity acquisition and formation. It may also give way to other essential forces, such as opportunity, resource, and social support (Caughey, 2006; Cownie, 2004; Di Leo, 2003; Engvall, 2003; Graham, Emery, & Hall, 2012; Halvorsen & Nyhagen, 2011; Piper, 1992; Talburt, 2000; Tomlinson, 2013; Whitchurch & Gordon, 2010).

Suggestion 1: Dream big and dream often. People may tell you that you dream in reaction to the structural constraints you face in your environment, that you do not dream if everything comes your way, that you dream only when you are unable to achieve what you desire, and therefore that it is useless to dream. Take a different view. Dreaming is the fountain of life. You go where you dream. You are what you dream of. As a scholar, you need to constantly resist becoming secular, practical, and vulgar. Always keep within yourself a level of naïveness, innocence, and dreaminess. Dream to be a revolutionary thinker whose mission is to change the way people live their lives. Dream to be a productive scholar who publishes one article a month and one book a year. Dream to be unique and different so that you see what other people do not see and discover what other people are not able to find. Dream to be a master instructor who can inspire students with knowledge. Your dreams provide motivation for you to do the best you can in the building of your scholarly identity. Your dreams also set standards for what you do in the development of your academic career.

Suggestion 2: Be a dwarf doer while aiming to be a giant achiever. You build your scholarly identity as you would build a sculpture. You do not and cannot finish it overnight. You need to take time and do one thing at a time. Be meticulous, punctual, and tenacious. There may be better days when you achieve much and bad days when you are not able to do as much as you hope for. Be ready to entertain feelings of frustration, disappointment, failure, hopelessness, and self-pity from time to time. The key to ultimate success is that you are devoted, you do not give up, and you persevere in every particular project you pursue as well as in the general career goal you attempt to attain. With care and effort on a gradual and consistent basis, you will surely create something in your name in the world of knowledge and scholarship.

Suggestion 3: Be a focused specialist while staying on track to be a generalist. At the end of your career, you may feel you are a generalist. You have traveled to the major areas of your discipline. You have gathered an extensive knowledge of all the fundamentals, from methods, theories, and areas of concentration, to issues of challenge, in the disciplinary domain. But at each stage of your career journey, do not even attempt to know everything. Do not claim to know everything. Do not appear to be knowledgeable on a wide range of issues. Delve fully into your specialty. Concentrate on what you are exploring, experimenting with, or writing about at each project. Turn off your interest in seemingly related but essentially irrelevant issues. It does not hurt to appear ignorant, absentminded, or really illiterate on many matters, even some of those that are taken for granted as basic knowledge in your discipline. Remember you are not a knowledge connoisseur. You do not entertain yourself with the idea that you are a knower. You are a knowledge discoverer and creator. You drive yourself with a self-image of not knowing.

Suggestion 4: Be a one-sided radical while gearing to become a well-rounded moderate. You may want to be a noncontroversial, well-balanced, and well-respected figure in your field. But you also understand that the balance or respect an ultimate moderate is able to command builds upon the breadth and depth he or she achieves in the creation and maintenance of opposing sides, issues, or schools of thought in a field. Do not begin as a moderate. Blast off instead as a radical. Roar up as a radical as well. The further you go in one track of thought, in one methodological approach, or in one line of argument, the more you will be able to understand the other way of thinking, reasoning, and analysis. The deeper and longer you are involved in a crossfire in your discipline, the richer and more meaningful your contributions as well as your career will be when you emerge as the ultimate moderate from the crossfire.

Suggestion 5: Be a contented everyday person while struggling as a never-satisfied scholar. You constantly strive for creative ideas, theories, methods, or techniques in your discipline. You plow through the literature. You reason backward and forward along a particular track of thought. You test and retest a new procedure or a new way of research. You write and rewrite your drafts. You are seldom satisfied in your pursuit of excellence in scholarship. With a high level of alertness in the academic domain, you are likely to be casual, relaxed, easy-going, carefree, or absentminded in many aspects of your life. But if you have a moment to think about how you live your life, just be content. Eat well. Dress well. Sleep well. Exercise as much as you can. Everything else, leave the way it is. Accept some disorder, frustration, pain, regret, and unhappiness in your life. Tolerate difference, discrepancy, and disruption. Be ready for surprises and the unexpected, such as misunderstanding, mistreatment, punishment, failure, injury, loss, and sickness. You may say to yourself from time to time: "Let God take care of it."

CONCLUSION

It is clear that career-making in postmodern academia is not just an individual endeavor. It involves three basic agents and agencies: academicians and their actions, institutions and their requirements, and the larger social structure and its dynamics.

As far as academicians are concerned, they choose to make a scholarly career. In their career pathway, they attend school, learn knowledge and skills, and obtain degrees. They search for academic jobs, affiliate with universities, research institutes, and other groups, and pursue scholarship in organizational settings. They seek professional contacts, network with funding sources, publication outlets, and service communities, and develop scholarly visibility in the academic circle. From a structural point of view, academicians build their individually unique career identity by obtaining degrees, securing positions, publishing products, teaching classes, presenting findings, serving others, competing for grants, winning awards, maintaining membership in scholarly associations, and earning tenure with an academic employer. Thus, degrees, positions, publications, teaching portfolios, presentations, service records, grants, awards, association involvement, and tenure combine to indicate how successful a career-making academician is in his or her lifetime journey or how productive an academic career is as a whole.

Along their career paths, academicians explore ways and means to avoid mistakes, failures, and disappointments. They strive hard for correctness, rightness, success, and pride. In this volume, specific suggestions are provided for academicians as they approach each milestone or major element in their academic career, from graduate school, job search and change, work and employment, networking, publishing, teaching,

Navigating the Academic Career:
Common Issues and Uncommon Strategies, pp. 131–133
Copyright © 2013 by Information Age Publishing
All rights of reproduction in any form reserved.

service, and association involvement, to tenure. Although an academician may find a particular suggestion helpful and useful, he or she should always understand that nothing applies to everyone at all time and in all occasions. Something that is effective at the present may not work in the future. Someone who shines today may not succeed tomorrow. An academic career in the contemporary era is an utterly open process. Career-making in postmodern academia is a constantly evolving effort. Each day is a new day. Each project is a new project. Academicians should always remain open yet selective, suspicious yet receptive, and critical yet accommodative to all new ideas, new methods, new theories, new suggestions, different trains of thought, and different ways of acting throughout their career journey.

Institutions provide training grounds, supply jobs, and offer media for career-making academicians. They establish standards, set rules, and impose requirements upon scholarly processes. They conduct assessments, evaluations, and judgments that are essential to personal motivation, academic productivity, occupational mobility, and self-identity. They control resources, opportunities, and rewards that are key to task performance, job success, professional accomplishment, and self-fulfillment. A few elite universities send their graduates to high-ranking institutions, placing them in a network that affords them prestigious points of contact for top-rated funding, sponsorship, research projects, and publication outlets. A multitude of ordinary programs, on the other hand, dispose of their students anywhere in the labor market or the knowledge enterprise without much regard for whether they can do something, work for a living, or just survive as an academic professional. Whereas institutions with high concentrations of talents may simply focus on productivity, quality, success, and merit, institutions of more ordinary performers may often falter in individual stagnation, interpersonal envy, group conflict, political friction, and overall mediocrity. In sum, institutions provide material conditions, spiritual sentiment, and a general environment in and by which career-making academicians work toward their career actualization in scholarship. A basically ordinary person may soar skyward if he or she happens to become part of a privileged network in a supportive institutional environment. An essentially brilliant person may disintegrate if he or she happens to fall into a destructive relationship in a swampy organizational milieu.

Following academicians in their career journey, institutions may eagerly recruit the bright, meticulously cultivate the promising, generously maintain the productive, and creatively promote the exceptional. They may also intentionally exclude the talented, maliciously abuse the innocent, unfairly treat the achiever, and ruthlessly persecute the innovator. Institutions and institutional practices vary tremendously in every aspect, from effectiveness, efficiency, productivity, rationality, fairness, and openness, to supportiveness. In view of academic careers and career-making scholars, new ideas and measures need to be constantly explored to reform and improve organizational system, operation, and service. In fact, only when existing tradition, system, and practice are questioned, can reform and renovation become a natural theme for all academic institutions in their drive for scholarly excellence and organizational efficacy.

The large social structure supports the knowledge enterprise because it consumes knowledge. It supplies resources for scholarly institutions because it needs academic personnel. The social structure expands in scale and scope as more and more academic institutions come into existence. The social process perpetuates itself as more and more career-making academicians flock to the knowledge enterprise with creative input and effective output. Social authority, control, and dominance increase while individuals and individuality become less important, insignificant, and negligible. Although no single academic institution, much less any individual academician, is able to curb, abort, or even reverse the general social process, its development or trend, every scholarly agent and agency should stay alert and be aware of the negative cycle in postmodern academia. A positive cycle is never impossible: The more career-making academicians there are, the more they contribute, the stronger the knowledge enterprise is to become; and the stronger the knowledge enterprise becomes, the more support the academic establishment is able to provide for its individual participants, the more career-seekers are to be attracted, motivated, and encouraged to make greater and more varied contributions.

In all, this volume serves its purpose if some of its readers, whether they are ordinary career-making professionals, powerful stakeholders in academic establishments, or keen observers and advocates of science and scholarship, say it makes them think again about what they do, how they operate in organizational settings, and how they relate to knowledge, the knowledge enterprise, and larger social dynamics.

APPENDIX

Documentation of basic acts and deeds is important for self-reference and peer review in the career of an academician. Presentation of essential achievements and contributions is critical as a scholar climbs an institutional ladder, creates a public impression, develops a professional identity, and charters a lifetime journey in the academic landscape. Below is an example that might help individual scholars in their documentation and presentation efforts.

Navigating the Academic Career:
Common Issues and Uncommon Strategies, pp. 135–179
Copyright © 2013 by Information Age Publishing
All rights of reproduction in any form reserved.

PROFESSIONAL INFORMATION FILE

CURRICULUM VITAE

PROFESSIONAL PREPARATION

Formal Education in All Three Domains of Human Knowledge
Doctoral Education
Postdoctoral Training

TEACHING EFFECTIVENESS/INSTRUCTIONAL CONTRIBUTIONS

History
Courses Taught
Teaching Philosophy
Teaching Goals and Objectives
Teaching Methods and Innovations
Academic Advisement and Mentoring
Teaching Research
Instructional Services
Efforts Made to Accommodate the Diverse Needs of Students
Student Evaluations
Peer Evaluations

CONTRIBUTIONS TO THE FIELD OF STUDY

History
Research Goals and Objectives
Publications
Presentations
Research Projects
Manuscript and Grant Reviews
Professional Conference Organization

CONTRIBUTIONS TO THE UNIVERSITY AND COMMUNITY

History
Service Philosophy
Service in the Department
Service in the College
Service in the University

Service to the Community
Service to the Profession

PROFESSIONAL AND PERSONAL RESPONSIBILITIES

PROFESSIONAL PREPARATION

Formal Education in All Three Domains of Human Knowledge
Doctoral Education
Postdoctoral Training

Formal Education in All Three Domains of Human Knowledge

I received formal education and hold academic degrees in all three domains of human knowledge, from the natural sciences, to the humanities, and to the social sciences.

From 1979 to 1983, I studied XXX at XXX University, one of the most prestigious universities in XXX. With extensive coursework in chemistry, mathematics, and physics, I obtained a Bachelor of Science degree in 1983.

From 1983 to 1986, I studied XXX at XXX University. Besides my concentration in history and philosophy of science and technology, I read major philosophers and thinkers in Eastern and Western civilizations, including Confucius, Kant, Hegel, Marx, Russell, and Mao. I obtained a Master of Art degree in 1986.

From 1989 to 1994, I studied XXX at the University of XXX. With extensive training in theories and research methods, I received a Master of Art degree in 1993 and a Doctor of Philosophy degree in 1994.

Formal education in all three domains of human knowledge has laid a broad and firm foundation for my academic career. I am not only programmed to take an analytical, comprehensive, and systematic approach to issues in my academic work, but also prepared to substantiate it with thorough analysis, solid evidence, and extensive knowledge.

My educational training is clearly evident in my academic work. In teaching, students comment gratefully on my broad knowledge base, as seen in officially administered anonymous evaluations. In research, I have published serious work on a wide range of issues, from urban housing to rural crime, from economic development to political democratization, from organizational behavior to social control, and from cultural change in XXX to social problems in the United States.

Doctoral Education

I worked on my PhD in XXX, with concentrations in XXX, at the University of XXX from 1989 to 1994. My doctoral work was academically and financially supported by the XXX Center.

The University of XXX is a major state university with a fine tradition of research and teaching. The XXX program at XXX has produced a number of reputable doctoral graduates, such as widely acclaimed criminologist XXX and sociologist XXX. The XXX Studies program at XXX is one of the best in the world.

The XXX Center is an internationally renowned institution for research and cultural exchange. Established by the United States Congress, it has been a vital academic entity to the mutual understanding among people and nations in XXX.

The academic climate at the University of XXX and the XXX Center fostered my early academic growth. I started presenting papers to professional conferences in the second year of my doctoral study. I published one of my research essays in a peer-review journal in the fourth year. By the time I received my PhD, I already had made fifteen professional presentations, published two papers, and had a few more accepted for publication.

I was nominated by my graduate committee for the Dissertation Competition at the National Council of Graduate Studies in 1994.

I won the Second Worldwide Competition for Young XXX sponsored by the International XXX Association in 1994.

Most important, I published my dissertation as a book. Only about five percent of dissertations are published as books in the United States.

Postdoctoral Training

I received postdoctoral training in the study of crime, deviance, and substance abuse at the University of XXX from 1995 to 1997. My postdoctoral fellowship was provided by the National Institute on Drug Abuse (NIDA).

XXX is an internationally renowned research university. The XXX Drug Abuse Research Center is a leading research organization on drug abuse in the country. It is one of only a few sites for institutional training grants sponsored by the National Institute on Drug Abuse.

My postdoctoral training included three major components: academic foundation, project participation, and grant experience. I attended weekly academic seminars given by seasoned scholars who specialize in various aspects of drug abuse research, from etiology to prevalence, from prevention to treatment, from policy to practice, and from theory to methodology. I engaged in weekly discussion groups among pre- and postdoctoral fellows, exchanging ideas and experiences in research, writing, presentation, publication, grant application, and job hunting.

I participated in two NIDA-funded and two State-of-XXX-supported projects. I formulated research plans, prepared questionnaires, conducted fieldwork, coordinated interviews, supervised data entry, performed data analysis, and wrote project reports, in cooperation with other members of each project.

I attended an intensive grant-writing workshop sponsored by the National Institute on Drug Abuse. I participated in several anatomic seminars on major forms of grants, by type, by private versus public source, and by success or failure. I reviewed multimillion grants for the United States Department of Health and Human Services.

I received both the Director's Travel Award and the Office of AIDS Travel Award from the National Institute on Drug Abuse.

Postdoctoral training has given me a wealth of knowledge and experience in funded research, from grant application to human subject protection, from research design to project management, from data analysis to academic publication, and from personnel supervision to maintaining constructive relationships with the funding agency.

Postdoctoral training is not common for PhD recipients in the social sciences. According to some expert estimates as well as reflected by employment bulletins published by the American XXX Association, the American Society of XXX, and the Academy of XXX Sciences, less than five percent of doctoral graduates in XXX have the opportunity to receive formal postdoctoral training at credible academic institutions, before they assume tenure-track assistant professorship in universities.

TEACHING EFFECTIVENESS AND INSTRUCTIONAL CONTRIBUTIONS

History
Courses Taught
Teaching Philosophy
Teaching Goals and Objectives
Teaching Methods and Innovations
Academic Advisement and Mentoring
Teaching Research
Instructional Services
Efforts Made to Accommodate the Diverse Needs of Students
Student Evaluations
Peer Evaluations

History

I started university teaching in 1986. I have taught for twenty six years in my academic career.

I have taught 26 different courses in XXX, XXX, XXX, XXX, and XXX. I have served thousands of students, undergraduate and graduate, on six different university campuses in two countries.

In 1986, I joined the faculty at XXX University of Science and Technology, one of the leading universities in XXX. I became a lecturer in 1988, three and half years before the normal five years of service required.

In 1994, I conducted my first class in XXX at the University of XXX. As part of my doctoral and postdoctoral training in teaching, I taught XXX, XXX, and XXX for the Department of XXX and XXX and XXX for the XXX Management Institute.

From 1996 to 1997, I taught five different courses in XXX, XXX, and XXX at XXX University and XXX University.

In 1997, I joined the faculty at XXX. During my tenure at XXX, I have taught twelve different courses, from general education courses to graduate seminars, from XXX core courses to option foundation courses, from theoretically oriented courses to practice-based internships, for two different options in XXX, as well as for the XXX program at XXX College of Extended Learning.

I have served a total of 5072 students, young and old, male and female, white and nonwhite, undergraduate and graduate, traditional and nontraditional, on job and off job, part-time and full-time, and representing a wide spectrum of socioeconomic status.

My instructional contributions at XXX are extraordinary and exceptional in terms of the number of students served, the number of courses taught, the variety of subjects involved, the level of education concerned, the mode of training applied, student reactions, and peer evaluations.

Courses Taught

A chronological list begins with the most recent.

By teaching large-enrollment courses in different subjects, at different levels, and for different options, I have made valuable contributions to the XXX program in particular and the University mission in general.

Teaching Philosophy

Teaching is my sacred duty as a university professor. I stand passionately and energetically in the forefront of classroom instruction. I teach different subjects at our full teaching load because I want to contribute the most I can to spreading knowledge to the larger population as well as to future generations. I teach large classes amid the challenge of student diversity and under-preparation because I want to contribute the most I can to using the power of knowledge to improve individual life and general social conditions.

I believe in and adhere to the following principles in teaching.

A Broad and Solid Knowledge Base

With a firm grounding in theory and methods as well as a broad knowledge base in various issues, I freely discuss with students different subject matters inside and outside the classroom.

Research-Based Teaching

With an active research agenda and a wide range of publication experiences, I share freely with students new ideas, new methods, and new findings in the forefront of knowledge.

Students are highly involved when I talk about my work on crime, deviance, social control, organizational behavior, higher education, and the academic career. Students are amazed when I advise and encourage them to improve their work by professional standards in presentation and publication.

A number of students, especially graduate students, have personally expressed their admiration for my clear writing styles and strong publication records.

Cooperative Learning
I follow an unassuming teaching style. I encourage students to learn from each other. I embrace enlightenment from students as well.

Cooperative learning especially suits students on our campus who often-times feel intimidated by the establishment of the knowledge enterprise and need external support to access the higher education system. In my classes, I treat students as partners. I encourage them, involve them, allow them to express themselves, and make them feel they have made to the point of understanding something important on their own. Comments by students in officially administered anonymous evaluations are illustrative: "Even if your verbal answer is incorrect, he does not make you feel inferior, he wants you to expand and think about the answer you just gave."

Interdisciplinary Approach
With formal training in natural sciences, the humanities, and social sciences, I automatically take an interdisciplinary approach to the organization and delivery of course materials.

International and Comparative Perspective
With experiences in different cultures and social systems, I habitually take a comparative perspective to the preparation and interpretation of course contents.

Multicultural Orientation
I am a culturally sensitive person. I fully understand and make every effort to meet the diverse learning needs of students.

Teaching Goals and Objectives

I focus on the following areas in teaching.

Understanding
I make every effort in class lectures and individual consultations to help students understand major concepts, ideas, and theories in a subject. I embrace the painstaking task of reasoning and understanding.

Fundamental Skills
I emphasize training students with essential skills in reading, presentation, and writing. The content of a subject changes from time to time. Students have to constantly connect to the educational system to update their knowledge. But how do we make them feel motivated and competent in their lifelong connection to education? We need to teach them essential skills that remain relatively stable over time but are key to job performance and continuing learning.

I have developed a course planning procedure and an instructional mechanism by which I am able to variably adjust, gradually implement, and effectively measure training and practice in reading, writing, and presentation in accordance with students' backgrounds, learning needs, and career goals. For example, I use a step-by-step monitoring system to ensure that students read and understand substantive course materials; I use an audience-in-charge format to motivate students to present in a professional manner; and I share with students my publications to establish the importance of writing and writing clearly in their minds.

Application
I train students to apply existing concepts and theories to real-world situations so that they can develop a better understanding of both theory and practice, and a higher ability to improve theorizing and social reality.

Outcome Assessment
I emphasize assessing the outcomes of student learning and using feedback to improve the ongoing process of teaching. I do not just make assignments, run class activities, and grade students into a normal distribution of success and failure. I care about what students have learned, how much they have learned, and whether they are able to use the knowledge learned to better themselves in work and life. My intent and effort reflect well in comments by students in officially administered anonymous evaluations. Among things they like most about me as an instructor, they indicated: "enthusiasm about students learning" and "cares about what students should know."

Teaching Methods and Innovations

I actively explore and experiment with various effective methods in teaching.

Lecture
I use standard lectures to help students understand major concepts, theories, methods, studies, patterns, and trends in a subject. I draw diagrams, develop outlines, raise questions, ask students to give examples, and inspire them to draw upon their own experience.

Discussion
In research seminars, I give students questions essential to the subject, divide them into small discussion groups where they work together to search for answers, and have them select a leader to present their collective answers. I then analyze their answers for completeness, strength, and weakness, and give them my point of view on the questions.

Presentation
Presentation is a fundamental skill. How do we make students improve their presentation skills and share their ideas effectively with others in class?

I encourage students to present their research project, a chapter summary, a concept anatomy, a theory analysis, a research briefing, and a theme topic in a subject; I allow students to present for five, ten, and fifteen minutes in duration; I make students present without evaluation, with evaluation from the instructor only, and with evaluations from fellow students, on content, organization, clarity, and mannerism. I have gathered useful data from these various experimentations.

Reading
Reading is another fundamental skill. How do we ensure that students read course materials and internalize the scientific way of thinking?

I make students present chapter reviews or an in-depth research into a concept, theory, or study covered in the text. I ask students questions in class. I use discussion groups. Most essentially, I give students quizzes every week or miniexams every three to four weeks.

Routine monitoring through weekly quizzes or miniexams works extremely well although it demands a tremendous amount of time, energy, and commitment from me as the instructor.

Writing

Writing is still another fundamental skill. How do we help students write and put their thoughts into words clearly and with confidence?

I give students essay exams in which they have to write six one-to-two-page essays in two to three hours. I ask students to write five-page theme essays. I require students to write research papers. I make students write abstracts for journal articles.

Most innovatively, I make students write book reviews and chapter additions to a book. A book review is a unique form of writing. In the context of training, it gives students dual benefits: reading another book besides the required textbooks and writing a commentary that is interesting and assertive. To my surprise, some of the book reviewers by students meet the standard of publication.

Inspiration from the Real World

I make arrangement for guest speakers to come to my classes. I ensure that students learn academic concepts and materials with a sense of reality.

Among guest speakers to my classes are sergeants from the University Police Department; the Substance Abuse Program Coordinator and her youth clients from the Covenant House of XXX; the Program Director, Program Counselor, and their clients from the New Directions for Youth in XXX Valley; and the Deputy Chief of XXX Police Department.

Service Learning in the Community

I implement service learning in my classes following the recent trend in college and university teaching.

I attend various sessions or workshops on service learning at the Annual Continuum of Service-Learning Conference, the XXX Teacher Scholar Summer Institute, and the XXX Center for Community-Service Learning.

I work closely with the XXX Center for Community-Service Learning, the XXX Probation Liaison, and the XXX Career Center in the process of implementation.

From weekly service-learning journals and final project reports by students, I gather the following comments: "I found the service-learning aspect of this course extremely beneficial"; "Using the skills obtained from this class has also improved the quality of my work. I have learned different terms and techniques to develop my job positively. I've also gotten compliments from my boss, she thinks I have improved my terminology and interviewing by a great deal"; and "the service learning journal is arguably some of the best work I have produced while at XXX. Also, I would like to take this opportunity to personally thank you for what has been a very fruitful semester. I thoroughly enjoyed being a part of your class."

Academic Advisement and Mentoring

I make myself available to students for general and specific advice in classrooms and during my office hours. I serve on thesis/dissertation committees for graduate students on and off campus.

Course-Related Advisement
I offer different office hours so that students have their choice of time to talk to me over the phone or visit me in office.

I call students whenever I have received a message from them. I talk to internship and service-learning supervisors to monitor student progress in various internship and service-learning agencies.

I offer students strategies and tactics to improve their performance on in-class quizzes and exams; I teach them how to conduct literature review; I prepare them for their class presentations; I make comments and corrections on their draft papers; I review and evaluate their general progress; I offer them advice on how to manage time, how to read for general knowledge, how to improve study skills, and how to specialize in a field of study.

General Advisement and Mentoring Activities
I do routine graduate checks for students. I check their records, advise them to develop a realistic plan, and encourage them to move forward with their professional pursuits.

I regularly receive students who seek advice on job search and graduate studies. I provide them with information and offer them specific advice on resume writing, GRE/GMAT/LSAT preparation, and graduate school application. Per their request, I write students letters of recommendation for their job, scholarship, and graduate school applications.

In the weeks of both winter and summer breaks, students often line up at my office for various kinds of advisement when I am the only one or one of a few fulltime faculty members available to students.

I sometimes receive calls from schoolteachers about course materials, media reporters about problem behavior, and local residents about their troubled children. I answer their questions with professional details, send materials when necessary, and give them specific directions as where to search for more information.

Special Advisement and Mentoring Activity I

As one of the core faculty members in XXX Option II: XXX, I continuously contribute ideas and thoughts to the improvement of the option curriculum, regularly advise students in the option, and routinely seek community connections for job opportunities and internship sites for students.

When I serve on the Graduate Comprehensive Examination Committee in XXX, I contribute ideas and thoughts to the organization of examination materials, write questions, give specific directions to students who plan to take the examination, grade examinations, and work with other committee members on final judgment by the committee.

As a member or the chair of individual graduate thesis committees, I send students packages of materials for reading and research. I sit with students for hours to help them design research, search for literature, develop theoretical arguments, and organize findings. I also work with other committee members on both administrative and academic matters so that students can navigate smoothly through the major milestones in their graduate project.

Special Advisement and Mentoring Activity II

I create opportunities for senior undergraduate students and graduate students to acquire teaching and research skills, to improve their employment prospects, and to foster their professional growth.

With funding from the College of XXX, I involved several undergraduate and graduate students in my research projects. Under my direct supervision, the students learned valuable skills in interviewing, data transcription, data analysis, literature review, and research generalization.

I coach the graduate and senior undergraduate students whom I invite to lecture in my classes. Student lecture offers an excellent learning opportunity for students, both behind the podium and in the audience. For student lecturers behind the podium, they learn how to work in teams, how to present a topic professionally, and how to translate their academic understanding into effective performance in teaching. For students in the audience, they are not only informed of a subject in a perspective similar to theirs, but also inspired to do the same or better when they themselves reach the same stage of academic growth.

I encourage graduate and senior undergraduate students in my classes to improve their written work for presentation and publication in professional media. I spend hours to offer them specific advice and assistance in writing, revision, and submission.

I solicit presentation proposals from students for the annual meetings of major academic associations, including XXX Association, Pacific XXX Association, Midwest XXX Society, and the Academy of XXX Sciences. I apply for travel funding for presenting students from various sources.

Special Advisement and Mentoring Activity III
I served on the Doctoral Advisory Committee for XXX at the University of XXX. I read his papers and dissertation thoroughly and provided him with detailed written comments. I participated in two oral defenses through telephone-conferencing. I was pleased to see Dr. XXX join the community of scholarship upon more than two years of intense work with him.

I served on the Master-level Advisory Committee for a number of XXX students at XXX College of XXX. As a member or the Chair of the thesis committee, I send students packages of materials for reading and research. I sit with students for hours to help them design research, search for literature, develop theoretical arguments, and organize findings. I also work with other committee members on both administrative and academic matters so that students can navigate smoothly through the major milestones in their graduate project.

Special Advisement and Mentoring Activity IV
I have been an active faculty mentor since 2004 for the Career Opportunity in Research, a program that is designed to train and prepare promising undergraduate students for doctoral-level academic work later in their professional career. The program is administered by the College of XXX at XXX under the auspices of the National Institute of Mental Health.

I served as a faculty mentor for Mr. XXX and Ms. XXX. I met with them weekly, up to ten hours a month. During our regular meetings, I offered advice on issues ranging from graduate school, career plans, study skills, research methodology, interviewing, theorizing, grant writing, conference presentation, research reports, and scholarly publishing, to teaching. Specifically, I trained them on teaching in some of my classes. I worked with them in developing research projects. I guided them through the human subjects review, coordination with local stakeholders in the community of research subjects, application of funding, development of research instruments, and other milestones typical of a primary research project. I edited, revised, and provided critical input on their conference abstracts as well as funding proposals they wrote under my mentorship. I took them to academic conferences and recommended them to summer undergraduate research programs at leading research universities. Mr. XXX is now a PhD candidate at XXX University.

Special Advisement and Mentoring Activity V

I offer academic advice and life-related assistance to visiting scholars and foreign students at XXX when they approach me or are referred to me by other sources.

In 2009-2010, for example, I served as a faculty advisor for three visiting scholars on XXX International Exchange Program: Professor XXX from XXX Finance and Economics College, and Mr. XXX and Mr. XXX from XXX Municipal Government. I received them numerous times in my office; I allowed them to audit my XXX, XXX, and XXX classes; I gave them books on police management, criminal justice, and organizational behavior; I searched information on municipal governments for them; I offered them comparative perspectives when they worked on their project reports; I took them to meet XXX County Department of Public Works officials; and I coordinated their visit to XXX Department of Transportation.

Currently, I am in contact with a number of visiting scholars on campus, offering them appropriate advice and support as requested. According to a recent survey by the Institute of International Education, XXX ranks the second among forty top XXX-level institutions in the nation as host for international students. I am glad that I have contributed my part to that record through my active involvement in the academic support for visiting scholars and foreign students on campus.

Special Advisement Activity VI

I am approached for academic advice and professional assistance from time to time by students and scholars across the country, mostly graduate students in major research universities, such as the University of Illinois at Champaign-Urbana, Indiana University at Bloomington, Rutgers University, and University of California at Irvine. They find me by my academic work and contact me through email or over the phone.

Some inquires involve a dozen of complex questions. For each inquiry, I carefully analyze its intent, search for academic references if necessary, and respond with technical details. One student wrote to me upon receipt of my written response: "... thanks for responding, again ... Your work definitely shaped large portions of my paper. I was relieved and pleased to be able to use it since it is so incredibly well written. You're awesome. Thanks again."

Teaching Research

Teaching is an important research topic by itself. On the basis of my teaching experimentation and innovation, I am actively pursuing research into teaching, its methods, effectiveness, general processes, institutional supports, and social impacts.

Peer-Refereed Publications on Teaching

A chronological list begins with the most recent.
(5) XXX. 1999. "Title of the Article." *College Teaching* 47.4: 153-157

My publications in pedagogy are well regarded by teaching scholars. I have received official invitations to speak to important teaching conferences in the country.

Professional Presentations on Teaching

A chronological list begins with the most recent.
(3) Title of the Presentation

Invited plenary presentation to the Third International Academic Conference of Young Scientists: Humanities and Social Sciences, XXX Polytechnic National University, Lviv, 2010

My presentations on teaching are well received in professional conferences or forums. I have received requests for copies of my papers from teaching professionals in different schools.

Session Organizer, Chair, and Discussant on Teaching and Learning

A chronological list begins with the most recent.
(1) Session Organizer, Chair, and Discussant, "Teaching, Research, and Service in Higher Education," the annual meeting, Pacific XXX Association, San Diego, 2012

Research-Based Course Material

I write course materials, including standard lecture notes, essay topics, and multiple-choice questions, on the basis of my teaching research.

By participating in professional conferences, making scholarly presentations, and publishing research papers on teaching, I have made valuable contributions to pedagogy beyond classroom instruction.

Instructional Services

I am actively involved in instructional services to improve teaching for both university professors and students.

Textbook Review
A chronological list begins with the most recent.
(1) Book Review, Routledge, 2012

I review textbooks because I want to play my part in quality control for college products. Specifically I want to give students quality academic materials to follow in their course work.

In each review, I read the manuscript thoroughly; I write detailed comments on each chapter; I write detailed comments on organization, coverage, writing, and other substantive matters; I make constructive suggestions for improvement. As applauded by the editors, my reviews are thoughtful, insightful, and extremely helpful.

Committee Service on Teaching
A chronological list begins with the most recent.
(9) Chair, Academic Planning Committee, College of XXX, XXX University, 2008-2009

I attend regular committee meetings; I contribute ideas and thoughts; I work on specific policy issues; I share my experiential observations as well as scholarly reflections on issues ranging from student preparation, educational access, effective teaching, and classroom interaction to the universal educational model and its impact on minority students.

In review of proposals, I carefully read each submission and write detailed comments on it; I express my positions effectively and always serve as a critical force in shaping the committee's final decision; and from time to time I write a whole letter or part of the justification for the committee recommendation to an upper agency.

Efforts Made to Accommodate the Diverse Needs of Students

I see myself as both a teacher and a person. I take into account real-world conditions in the lives of students and make every effort to facilitate the learning process for students.

Athletes

I give them time to review course materials; I allow them to retake a missed quiz or exam during my office hours.

I grade their quizzes one by one manually and enter scores on their records after the bulk of grading on the class is finished.

Students with Disabilities

I copy my lecture notes for them; I make arrangements for them to take quizzes or exams at the Center on Disabilities on campus; I give them more office time to help with their papers and presentations; I talk to some of the officers at the Disability Center to monitor their academic progress.

Students Caught in Emergencies

I comfort them with words over the phone; I allow them to make up the coursework they have missed due to emergencies.

General

I routinely gather useful information on conferences, competitions, job openings, internship or volunteer opportunities, scholarships, and graduate schools, and share it with students inside and outside the class.

Student Evaluations (Quantitative Scores)

Student reactions to my teaching are strong and highly positive. Formal scores from officially administered anonymous student evaluations are as follows:

Format I: By Semester

Spring, 2012
XXX course: Median 5.0; Mean 4.8

Fall, 2011
XXX course: Median 4.0; Mean 4.2

Format II: By Course
XXX Course
Fall, 2006: Median 4.7; Mean 4.6
Fall, 2005: Median 5; Mean 4.6

Student Evaluations (Qualitative Comments)

Student reactions to my teaching are strong and highly positive. Excerpts from officially administered confidential/anonymous student evaluations are as follows:

Knowledge
"Professor XXX displays mastery of his subject, and offers a challenging and constructive course which I enjoy very much"; "I appreciate the instructor's obvious knowledge about the subject"; "The professor is very knowledgeable in the course material and presents the information well"; "He is a very intelligent, respectful person with a fair grading scale and a wealth of knowledge"; "Instructor very knowledgeable and informative"; "The instructor is well educated in this subject"; "Teacher has great knowledge of course material"; "Very knowledgeable, better than many XXX professors"; "Knowledgeable, Organized, Clear"; "The instructor is well educated in this subject"; "Teacher has great knowledge of course material"; "Dr. XXX is very knowledgeable and interesting. He really knows his subject matter"; "Dr. XXX has an extremely definite knowledge of his material"; "He was very sincere and knowledgeable about what he was teaching"; "Have a sense of material in real life situation"; "His profound knowledge of the course matter made the class a very enjoyable experience"; "Thanks to the instructor I have come to understand theories and learned about sociological theorists"; "He has a lot to offer to our class and the students in general."

Lecture
"This class is informative, he gives us real examples. His lecture is easy to follow, and it's helpful. His speech pace is appropriate (not too fast or slow) so that it's easy to take notes"; "Great way of explaining the chapters"; "The professor is good when it comes to keeping the material clear and organized. I enjoyed taking his class ... "; "I like the way you teach, professor"; "I love your class, professor. I also like your teaching methods. I look forward to your lectures every Friday"; "Explains the instruction in great detail so that all students have an understanding"; "The instructor put information in the text in words that you can relate to"; "His ability to take difficult concepts and organize it in a manner that is clear and under-

standable"; "The lecture is easy to understand for me as an international student"; "Explains material elaborately. A+"; "Gives great examples that help the material understandable"; "Abilities to explain concepts concisely and clearly in class"; "Dr. XXX is very explicit, explains the information well. It's great to learn concepts from great sociologists"; "The lectures required students to be critical about social, political and economic issues"; "I am confident that this professor provides great lectures that are relevant to the subject matter"; "Professor XXX describes everything clearly so that the students are able to comprehend"; "The instructor made the class material clear and easy to understand even though the material had difficult content"; "Dr. XXX was very stimulating in his form of lecture"; "Dr. XXX explained each theorist clearly and made it easy for me to understand. After reading the text, I was confused, but Dr. XXX cleared it up for me"; "Dr. XXX seems to have a passion for teaching this subject and it comes out in his lecture."; "I enjoyed the unstructured sense of humor and calm teaching manner."

Class Interaction

"The professor is very enthusiastic and his love of the subject comes through. I like the way he injects humor into his lectures"; "The professor has a way of making the class entertaining … I enjoyed it"; "One time you acted out a scene between parents and a teenage delinquent all by yourself and it was great"; "Big Event was a wonderful learning experience for all. Dr. XXX handled the visitors perfectly"; "I felt that Professor XXX was very interesting and made the class fun to understand"; "The thing I liked best about the course is the group presentation on each chapter of the book. I believe it gives the students a chance to learn the material and share it with the other classmates"; "Makes the class interesting and very informative on the course topics"; "He brought in a panel from Covenant House. It was interesting to hear first-hand experience"; "The open discussion in lecture. The way he conducts the seminar"; "Encouraged students to work together in projects and classroom experience"; "Allows you to express your opinions"; "he likes to have everyone involved in the discussions"; "He put everyone at ease, made all of us feel comfortable"; "He encouraged and noted our improvements"; "The instructor is very candid and clear regarding what is expected"; "Offers help as well as guiding us to write term papers"; "The instructor friendly and open connection with entire class since it is a large class"; "The fact that the instructor is willing to adjust to the class problems with lecture and exams"; "The instructor make the course seem manageable when it's really difficult"; "He makes sure that everyone is on top of things."

Class Assignments

"I think the study guide outlines for each chapter were extremely help-ful"; "... really informative"; "He makes it clear when all assignments are due. It was a pleasure taking this class"; "Assignments are fair and educa-tional"; "I also like having a quiz every week. That way it gives us a chance to test while the material is fresh on our heads"; "Grading procedure was very fair"; "His quizzes are made understandable and fair"; "The quizzes kept me in track with the readings and lectures"; "I like how the instructor conducts his exams, giving the students time to prepare"; "The clarity of what is expected to be known for the tests"; "Weekly quizzes force you to keep up on readings and lectures to do well"; "Class assignments—very fair, a lot of positive reading"; "Tests are representative of materials cov-ered"; "He hands out the exams on time, and also he discusses the mate-rials well in class"; "He goes over quizzes after to make things clear"; "Tests are hard, but I think the grading is fair"; "His tests are clear and fair, there are no tricks"; "Dr. Shaw's method of testing is excellent not because I've gotten good grades but because we learn the material and practice it in essay tests and keep the knowledge in us"; "The instructor is fair in his dealing with students, in terms of grades, assignments, or hav-ing to talk on a one-to-one basis during office hours."

Relationship with Students

"Very passionate & knowledgeable"; He is excellent at responding emails right away"; "You are a funny man! Great class!"; "He motivates you to do better and not to stress"; "The instructor cares about the students and does everything to help them out"; "Emphasizes class unity, helping each other"; "Dr. XXX demonstrates concern for his student's progress"; "He was always punctual and on time. I really was impressed how he knows everyone's name in the class"; "He has time for his students after class"; "Treats students fairly"; "Dedication to class and students"; "He is very encouraging in offering assistance to students. Wants all students to feel empowered. Wants everyone to succeed"; "He was compassionate and truly cared for his students"; "Dr. XXX has a wonderful personality"; "Very good instructor in that he respects students as well as the students respect him"; "He's personable and relates to his students as individuals"; "He is very courteous and caters to the needs of his students"; "He cares about his students"; "The instructor is fair and very gracious"; "Commu-nicates well with students and cares"; "Instructor is extremely fair and understanding"; "Dr. XXX really cares about student progress and encourages visits to his office"; "Even if your verbal answer is incorrect, he does not make you feel inferior, he wants you to expand and think about the answer you just gave."

Overall

"I would definitely recommend this course to fellow students. Great class, awesome professor"; "Great professor!!!"; "Great instructor"; "Great class & subject matter. Instructor is first-rate!"; "XXX is a very great teacher and I would love to take another class with him because I learn a lot. I really looked forward to coming to class"; "From my experience in law enforcement, this course has provided me with a new insight that will positively influence my thoughts toward society"; "Dr. XXX's class is fun and enjoyable to attend. He takes the class seriously and is a committed professor"; "Dr. XXX teaches in a way which allows students to learn as well as do well. The class is 'relaxing' enough so that learning takes place, but as a student you always know what is expected of you. Some classes are, or can be so stressful that you don't learn because you are always stressed out about your final grade"; "Great overall!"; "Excellent!"; "He is a wonderful professor"; "Dr. XXX is an excellent teacher"; "His interactive teaching style ... knowledge on the subject ... timely return of paperwork/office hours availability"; "He is refreshingly different from other professors"; "Every Tuesday-Thursday morning I looked forward to coming to class"; "Dr. XXX shows a lot of passion when he teaches. It shows that he really likes these subjects and in turn, gives others the desire to like it too"; "I like coming to class because Dr. XXX is one of my top instructors"; "He is an excellent instructor and everyone should give themselves the opportunity to take his courses"; "This is the second class that I have taken with Dr. XXX and I enjoy his teachings still. His criminology and juvenile delinquency classes are extremely informative."

Student Evaluations (MPA Class)

Most of my MPA students are established career professionals. They range from city planners, county appraisers, a college information director, a school district financial manager, a county sheriff department's division chief, PhD holders, corporate officers, and private practitioners.

In a scale of 1 to 5 (excellent to very poor), most participants selected "1" or "excellent" for both "the course in general" and "the instructor" in the confidential/anonymous class evaluations. The ratings are consistent with written comments:

"This is an excellent course that applies directly to management in my workplace"; "This course was very well balanced between instruction by the professor and student participation. The class took the 'shared leadership' approach to instruction. Also, Dr. XXX's sense of humor lends itself well to the classroom setting"; "This course is my favorite thus far. The teachings were very relevant to organizational studies. I was very happy with the content and detail provided at each lecture"; "Good course, a must for one who is going to be in a management/administration position."

"I was very impressed by Dr. XXX. He is a great communicator, animated, and insightful. His examples and presentation manner made each class enjoyable. I look forward to enrolling in any other courses he may be teaching"; "Dr. XXX combined theory and practice very well. He allowed for very active discussion by all students. Overall, the class went very well"; "Your sense of humor in lectures added a significant amount of interest on the topics. Good job!"

"Dr. XXX is very personable. He is a great facilitator and really brought out in-depth discussion with all members' participation"; "Dr. XXX's understanding of research in this area and his expertise greatly enhanced my learning. He is well versed in both theoretical as well as practical application"; "Dr. XXX—knowledgeable, communicated well to class, enthusiastic, fantastic teacher, open to discussion, information relevant to subject, respectful of other's opinions. I highly recommend him. Would take another class from him."

"This is an excellent professor. I hope the university offers more courses with this professor. He facilitates knowledge, is very professional, and cares about his students. He listens objectively and helps us apply organizational behavior to each of our own settings. Bravo!"; "Dr. XXX actually cares about the students ... Atmosphere was great ... I hope MPA office acknowledges Mr. XXX for such hard work and his dedication"; "Dr. XXX is very thorough (too thorough at times) but overall an excellent professor who knows the subject matter ... I enjoyed and learned from his teachings and visions. The course is very applicable to my needs."

"Without reservation, Prof. XXX is one of the most passionate and caring instructors I have ever had the privilege to learn from. He is motivated and his depth of knowledge motivated me. I respect his professional demeanor and hope that others pay close attention to what he offers, because he is one of a kind!"

Student Reactions (A Formal Petition by XXX Students)

In the end of Fall, 2002, about 100 students filed a formal petition to the Chair of the XXX Department and the Dean of the College of XXX. They pleaded that I teach XXX.

For years, students in my XXX class ask me to teach XXX. I always responded by saying (1) it takes time to prepare a new course; and (2) they should take classes with different instructors to diversify their educational experience at XXX. But this time with a formal petition, they were really serious and insistent.

In their petition, students write: "We believe that Dr. XXX is an excellent professor. We trust him and learned much from his lecture and reading assignments. He has been an asset to us in our quest for training in XXX theory. He is able to relate the class material to the real world and our future careers."

Student Reactions (Anecdotes)

A few of my colleagues told me that students in their class speak highly about Dr. XXX and his classes. One of the colleagues said it is good to hear something positive from students when we so often see students complain openly in class.

Dr. XXX, Undergraduate Coordinator in XXX, writes "As Undergraduate Evaluator, I have received considerable input from students about Dr. XXX's teaching. In addition, his teaching evaluations affirm student's high opinions of his performance in the classroom."

One of my colleagues told me that one of her students owed it to Dr. XXX and his class as a primary source of inspiration when she asked her class, on the first day of instruction, who or what makes them interested in XXX.

One of my former colleagues at XXX in XXX told me that when she tried to get my office number over the phone, she heard from a student staff at XXX saying Dr. XXX is a wonderful professor and everybody likes him.

One of our Department staff told me that one of her classmates took my XXX class. She learned a lot from that class and liked it very much.

One of my XXX colleagues told me that a student escorting her to the parking lot said he learned most from Dr. XXX's class among all the classes he has taken at XXX.

While anecdotes do not qualify as representative evidence, they might still provide some indication of a general impression I have created among students on campus.

Peer Evaluations

I am recognized and respected for excellence in teaching by my colleagues. Some excerpts from peer evaluations are as follows:

Dr. XXX

"Sound and thorough knowledge of subject matter"; "Excellent organization and presentation. Well-ordered with introduction and preview of main topics"; "Clarity of communication: Excellent. Clear and precise delivery"; "Organization and Syllabus: Excellent. Aims of course specified. Topics for each week identified"; "Instructor shows professional skills in every aspect of teaching."

Dr. XXX

"Dr. XXX was very enthusiastic about his presentation of ... He carefully went through the stages of Human Spirit... His illustrations and examples demonstrated he had a thorough knowledge of the subject. He was very dynamic and animated"; "Overall, I was impressed with Dr. XXX's organization of the topic, the classroom management, and the use of the blackboard. The level of presentation appeared appropriate for the students. He revealed enthusiasm about teaching and expressed concern about student learning."

Dr. XXX

"Professor XXX did an excellent job of connecting with the students in his Theory I class. This is particularly notable since theory tends to be, by definition, abstract and, therefore, difficult for student involvement"; "Professor XXX's lecture was clear, focused, and at the appropriate level for the material and students. The lecture was well developed"; "It was easy to take notes in Professor XXX's class since he talked clearly and used the board effectively"; "The course appears to be quite rigorous in approach."

Dr. XXX

"He is at ease in the classroom, confident in his pedagogical skills and substantive knowledge"; "His presentation was clear and coherent, following a logical and empirically grounded format. His presentation was well modulated and understandable. He set the level of discourse at an appropriate level—abstract enough, but also grounded in observation"; "A strong theoretical background undergirded his presentation. This was a very strong dimension of his lecture, to my mind."

Dr. XXX

"Dr. XXX had an excellent control of the class. While he presented the course materials in a theoretically powerful and intellectually stimulating way, he also tactically used pauses, jokes, and metaphors to keep the whole class involved"; "Dr. XXX demonstrated superb mannerism and skillfulness in eliciting class participation..."; "Dr. XXX exhibited an exceptional analytical skill in explaining abstract concepts and theories..."

Dr. XXX

"The class presentation was rigorous, detailed, and well thought out. New material was added on the board as the presentation proceeded. The sociological analysis was straight forward and presented in a way the students could follow"; "Dr. XXX was at ease with the students, and has a clear grasp of the material. He is committed to delivering a complex analysis to the students, and is accessible for questions and explanations. He gave careful responses to student questions and comments."

Dr. XXX

"... have been impressed with your knowledge, your argumentation, and your preparation. The manner in which you conduct your class is exemplary"; "The student interaction seems strong and positive, and student comments have generally been quite favorable."

CONTRIBUTIONS TO THE FIELD OF STUDY

History
Research Goals and Objectives
Publication
Presentation
Research Projects
Manuscript and Grant Review
Professional Conference Organization

History

Overall
I started serious scientific research in the third year of my undergraduate study at XXX University. I published my first research paper with my undergraduate mentor, Professor XXX, in Research Journal of XXX University in 1984.

In XXX, I have published 2 books (first author), 3 book chapters (editorial board member on 3 of the edited volumes), 3 research papers, and a number of newspaper articles.

In XXX, I have made 128 professional presentations to local, regional, national, and international academic conferences or forums in Asia, Europe, Oceania, North America, Latin America, and the Caribbean.

In XXX, I have published 5 books, 4 other book chapters, 1 book review, and 33 articles in peer-refereed journals.

At XXX
I have made 99 professional presentations to local, national, and international academic conferences or forums in Asia, Europe, Oceania, North America, and Latin America.

I have published 25 research articles in peer-refereed journals.

I have published three peer-refereed book chapters and one book review.

I have published four books, all of which have received positive reviews from established academic media, such as *Choice*, *Contemporary XXX*, and *The Review of Higher Education*. Besides a highly positive review from *The Review of Higher Education*, the 2004 book has been at the top of some academic advisor's list of books to read for postgraduate students and professionals. The 2002 book appeared in "Outstanding Academic Titles, 2003," *CHOICE: Current Reviews for Academic Libraries*.

Research Goals and Objectives

Research is my way of life. I conscientiously pursue research amid my full teaching schedule because I embrace a profound intellectual passion to understand human civilizations and to improve social life through understanding. I wholeheartedly seek publication outlets for my research products because I want to make my best contributions to knowledge as it moves along with human progress.

As a XXX, I am primarily interested in the study of XXX, XXX, and XXX in relation to larger social system. I study XXX, XXX, and XXX in XXX, the XXX country embodying the spirit of Eastern civilizations. I study XXX, XXX, and XXX in XXX, the XXX society leading the way of progress in Western civilizations. By studying social problems in these two contrasting nations, I aim not only to better understand the diversity of human social evolutions, but also to bridge the East with the West toward an integrated communal world system.

As a teaching scholar, I am naturally concerned with the art of pedagogy. Creating knowledge is essential to human progress. Spreading knowledge is by no means less important because it not only determines how knowledge is used, but also affects how knowledge is produced in the future. With this concern in mind, I also spend time on teaching research as well.

Publication

Book
A chronological list begins with the most recent.
(3) XXX. 2004. Title of the Book. XXX, MD: XXX Publishing Group

This volume examines academic careers and career-making endeavors in contemporary society. It serves as a critical forum for theoretical reflection and generalization, a thought-provoking reference for institutional innovation and reform, and a down-to-earth guide for individual learning and practice. Specifically, the volume first explores the key requirements for academicians to make a career, including educational preparation, job searching, institutional placement, and professional networking. It then identifies the essential elements for scholars to build and maintain a career identity, from the degree, position, publication, teaching, presentation, service, grant, award, and membership in academic associations to tenure. Delving into the consequences of career-making in postmodern academia, the volume explores how seemingly impulsive individual potential and actions translate into socially effective forces, and how established social forces and institutions dominate, manipulate, and oppress creativity and productive endeavors.

This book is published in October, 2004 by XXX Publishing Group, "one of the largest and fastest growing independent publishers and distributors in North America." XXX Publishing Group publishes over more than twenty imprints in all fields in the humanities and social sciences, distributed through its own National Book Network, "North America's second largest distributor of independent trade book publishers." "More than 20,000 new books have been published since the company was founded in 1975."

Listing. This book stands at the top of the List of Books to Read for Postgraduate Students and Professionals by some academic advisors, followed by _Career Strategies for Women in Academia: Arming Athena, Ms. Mentor's Impeccable Advice for Women in Academia, An Author's Guide to Scholarly Publishing_, and _Successful Publishing in Scholarly Journals: Survival Skills for Scholars_.

Review. This book receives a highly positive review from the prestigious _Review of Higher Education_ by The Johns Hopkins University Press.

"Like those students, I found myself similarly situated several years ago when I contemplated jumping head first into the academy. How I wish someone could have given me XXX's XXX. It's the type of book you want to thrust into the hands of every student who sits in your office and says, 'I'm thinking of getting my PhD and teaching at the college level' or every junior faculty member who walks through the door."

"Thankfully, XXX ... offers for everything from successful publishing and researching guidelines to managing departmental politics. Much of his advice rings true and is not the usual stuff of advice columns in publications like The _Chronicle of Higher Education_. Good professional advice like this only comes by way of a competent and caring mentor. Sadly, such mentors are often in short supply. XXX offers needed guidance in an easy-to-access manner."

"XXX explores this landscape without preaching, romanticizing, or condemning it. It is this straightforward delivery and thoughtful analysis that makes XXX a book you want to put in everyone's hands and keep on your shelf for easy reference."

—The Review of Higher Education

Peer-Refereed Journal Article
A chronological list begins with the most recent.
(2) XXX. 2010. "Title of the Article." *Journal of XXX* 26.1: 53-71

This article studies the XXX correctional system with respect to its history, organizational structure, legal framework, practice, management, and operational effectiveness. It represents one of the first systematic efforts in the academic literature to identify, categorize, and analyze correctional institutions and practices in XXX as the country undergoes economic reform and social transformation in an unprecedented scale.

Journal of XXX is an international peer-refereed journal in criminology and criminal justice. With aim at "a cogent, thorough, and timely exploration" of each topic, the journal has provided "authoritative, balanced examinations on a variety of critical issues in criminal justice today," from organized crime, community policing, gangs, white-collar crime, excessive police force, and corrections to comparative justice.

Journal of XXX maintains an international editorial board composed of leading figures in various areas of criminology and criminal justice. The board decides on critical themes and selects prominent scholars as guest editors to be in charge of each single-themed special issue.

Journal of XXX is published by Sage Publications, "an independent international publisher of journals, books, and electronic media." Known for its commitment to quality and innovation, Sage Publications is "a world leader in its chosen academic, educational, and professional markets."

Chapter Contribution
A chronological list begins with the most recent.
(1) XXX. 2010. "Title of the Chapter." Pp. 39-63 in *XXX*, edited by XXX, XXX, and XXX. Boca Raton, FL: CRC Press.

This article is selected for inclusion in *XXX*, a collection of critically important essays addressing key aspects of policing in a global community.

XXX is edited by leading scholars and practitioners in criminal justice, including the founding president of the International Police Executive Symposium, a well-known forum that "brings police researchers and practitioners together to facilitate cross-cultural, international and interdisciplinary exchanges for the enrichment of the policing profession."

Book Review
A chronological list begins with the most recent.
(1) XXX. 2009. Review of "XXX." *International Journal of XXX* 19.2: 226-227

Newspaper Article
A chronological list begins with the most recent.
(5) XXX. 2002. "Title of the Article." *XXX Economic Herald*: April 9

Presentation

Presentation: Invited Speech
A chronological list begins with the most recent.
(5) Title of the Presentation
Presented to an audience of academic staff and postdoctoral scholars, XXX University Institute, Florence, 2007

I was invited to give speeches to faculty, graduate trainees, and undergraduate students by major universities and academic institutions while traveling overseas. Among those XXX institutions where I spoke formally, XXX University, XXX University, and XXX University are three of the top ten universities in XXX.

My speeches in XXX foster positive understandings of both critical academic issues and American society by XXX youth and intellectuals. They raise visibility and distinction for XXX as an American institution of higher learning in one of the most important XXX societies in the world.

Presentation: International Conference
A chronological list begins with the most recent.
(3) Title of the Presentation
Presented to the 10th International XXX Convention, Durban, 2010

My presentations in major international conferences afford me important opportunities to share my research and thoughts with scholars from other social and cultural backgrounds. They raise visibility and distinction for XXX as an American institution of higher learning in both developing and developed societies around the world.

Presentation: National Conference
A chronological list begins with the most recent.
(1) Title of the Presentation
Presented to the annual meeting, American Society of XXX, St. Louis, 2008

My presentations in major national conferences afford me important opportunities to share my research and thoughts with scholars from other academic institutions. They raise visibility and distinction for XXX in scholarship and teaching around the country.

Presentation: Regional Conference
A chronological list begins with the most recent.
(1) Title of the presentation
Presented to the annual meeting, Midwest XXX Association, Minneapolis, 2012

My presentations in major regional conferences afford me important opportunities to share my research and thoughts with scholars from various comparable institutions. They raise visibility and distinction for XXX in scholarship and teaching in strategic regions of the country. They also help bring leadership role to XXX in some academic fields.

Research Projects

Funded Projects
With funding from the College of XXX and XXX Institute at XXX, I conduct research projects in the local community as well as overseas. I involve both undergraduate and graduate students in my research projects. Under my direct supervision, the students learned valuable skills in interviewing, data transcription, data analysis, literature review, and theoretical generalization

I make presentations to professional conferences on the basis of project findings. I publish peer-refereed articles and academic books upon completion of projects.

Individual Projects
I take research as a constant intellectual pursuit. In addition to the funded research, I have various self-initiated research and writing projects on my academic agenda.

Manuscript and Grant Review

I am routinely invited by publishers, journals, and funding agencies to review manuscripts and grants. I respond to them because I want to ensure that serious academic research is supported and that quality scholarly products are made available to play their part in enhancing human understanding as well as in improving general social conditions.

Journal Article Review
A chronological list begins with the most recent.
(1) Journal Reviewer, American Journal of XXX, 2011

In each review, I read the manuscript thoroughly; I make detailed comments throughout the manuscript; I make specific recommendations to the editor; I make constructive suggestions to the author(s). As applauded by the editors, my reviews are thoughtful, insightful, and reflective of most recent developments in the field.

Research Monograph Review
A chronological list begins with the most recent.
(8) Book Reviewer, Cambridge University Press, 1999

I read the manuscript thoroughly; I write detailed comments on each chapter; I write detailed comments on organization, coverage, writing, and other substantive matters; I make constructive suggestions to the author (s) for improvement. As applauded by the editors, my comments are thoughtful, insightful, and right to the point.

Grant Review
A chronological list begins with the most recent.
(1) Grant Reviewer, National Science Foundation, 2010

I read the grant proposal thoroughly; I write detailed comments; I make constructive suggestions to the applicants for improvement; and I make reasonable recommendations to the grant sponsor. As applauded by the grant officer, my comments are thoughtful and my recommendations are instrumental to the final award decision.

Textbook Review
A chronological list begins with the most recent.
(3) Book Reviewer, Wadsworth Publishing, 2009

I read the manuscript thoroughly; I write detailed comments on each chapter; I write detailed comments on organization, coverage, writing, and other substantive matters; I make constructive suggestions to the author (s) for improvement. As applauded by the editors, my comments are informative, insightful, and extremely helpful.

Professional Conference Organization and Service

I organized my first professional conference in the United States, the first Annual Conference on Issues of Culture and Communication in Asia and the Pacific, in 1991 when I was a degree associate at the XXX Center. Since then I have served many different roles, as organizing member, translator, moderator, discussant, and chair, in various professional conferences.

I participate in professional conference organization because I want to ensure that scholars are connected in their research, that new ideas and methods are shared in a timely manner, and that knowledge grows and spreads through continuing communications across disciplines.

Program Committee
A chronological list begins with the most recent.
(1)Member, Program Committee, the annual meeting, Pacific XXX Association, 2011-2012

I organize two invited sessions and two open sessions. I send letters of acceptance and coordinate visits to the conference by foreign speakers. I preside over four sessions and entertain invited speakers at appropriate receptions.

Session Chair
A chronological list begins with the most recent.
(2) Chair, Title of the Session, the 60th annual meeting, American Society of XXX, St. Louis, 2008

I introduce speakers; I provide thematic connections from presentation to presentation; I make critical comments on presentations; I take questions from the audience. With effective management, I ensure that sessions go smoothly and successfully in front of a highly active audience.

Session Discussant (while chairing the session)
A chronological list begins with the most recent.
(4)Discussant, XXX Forum on Science, Technology and Society, Harvey Mudd College, Claremont, 2008

I collect papers from speakers before the meeting; I read each paper thoroughly; I make detailed comments on each paper; I provide thematic connections among presentations at the session. Through serious work, I ensure that both speakers and participants learn and contribute not only for the specific success of a session but also to the general benefit of scholarship.

Session Organizer
A chronological list begins with the most recent.
(2) Session Organizer, the annual meeting, Midwest XXX Society, 2011-2012

I submit session proposals to the program committee; I receive, and solicit when necessary, papers from scholars in the field; I review and evaluate each submission; I send accepted papers to the program committee; I keep authors informed of the status of their submission as well as important dates pertaining to the meeting; I greet speakers personally at the meeting.

CONTRIBUTIONS TO THE UNIVERSITY AND COMMUNITY

History
Service Philosophy
Service in the Department
Service in the College
Service in the University
Service to the Community
Service to the Profession

History

Prior to XXX
Service has been part of my life since the start of my schooling. I served as class leader, school leader, and lead actor in the school troupe in elementary school, middle school, and high school.

I served as class leader and senior student advisor during my undergraduate and graduate studies at XXX University.

I was the founding President of XXX Association for Economic Development from 1983 to 1986. The association organized XXX County natives in greater XXX to contribute their talents to economic development back in their home county.

In 1988, I was invited by XXX Municipal Government to serve as a deputy head of its suburban XXX Township. I organized experts in urban planning, civil engineering, and chemical engineering from XXX University of Science and Technology and other academic institutions to provide advice to commerce and industry in the township.

During my doctoral study in XXX, I twice ran for systemwide student organization offices. I organized two large-scale student conferences. I served as student representative in the Institute of Culture and Communication Council at the XXX Center. I was Vice-President of the Graduate Students' Organization in the Department of XXX at the University of XXX. In addition, I volunteered for the Judiciary and Governor's Literacy Program in the State of XXX, as well as several private organizations, including XXX Health Center, XXX Congress of Science, and American Cancer Society.

At XXX, I served as Fellow Coordinator and XXX Liaison for the XXX Center. I invited seasoned scholars to speak to the Center's Monday Seminar. I also presided over a weekly discussion group among pre- and post-doctoral fellows. In addition, I reviewed articles for *Violence and Victims* and multimillion grants for the United States Department of Health and Human Services. I also provided research consultation for the XXX Group in Maryland.

At XXX

I started to serve on the university committee right in the beginning of my appointment, "before anyone knew it," commented by one of my colleagues.

In the Department of XXX, I have served as assessment liaison, option coordinator, facilitator for curriculum innovations, faculty representative in the major fair, faculty advisor for the student organization, program coordinator for the Honors Convocation, and chairs or members of various committees. Currently, I am the Chair of the Assessment Committee, one of the most important and labor-intensive committees in the department.

In the College of XXX, I have engaged in a range of service activities from being a faculty representative at the Open House to serving on the Workload Committee to working as a member of the Associate Dean Search and Screening Committee. Most important, I served as the Chair of the Academic Planning Committee from 2008-2009 after one year of cochairing the committee with a colleague from the Department of XXX in 2007-2008.

In the University, I have served on many campuswide committees. I have engaged in various other services as well. Recently, I serve as a Senator-at-Large at the Faculty Senate and a member of the Campuswide Advisory Board on the XXX Program at XXX College of Extended Learning. I was twice nominated for the Vice President of the Faculty Senate.

I have reviewed textbooks, research monograph, and journal articles in my field of study.

I have organized programs, moderated sessions, and served as discussant for professional conferences.

I have provided professional advice and comments to students across the country as well as residents and organizations in the local community in response to their specific needs and requests.

I actively seek for service opportunities. I fill out service forms every year to the Faculty Senate at XXX. I even send letters to the community, expressing my intent to serve their needs with my professional expertise. My service record is systematic, consistent, coherent, and comprehensive. It involves different activities at different levels in different organizational environments.

Service Philosophy

Service is an integral part of my academic life. As a responsible scholar, I always remain ready to answer calls from my profession, institution, and community for service. I review manuscripts and assume association duties because I want to contribute my part in keeping the vitality of academic disciplines and larger academia. I serve on departmental, college, and university committees because I want to contribute the most I can to promoting the spirit and practice of self-governance and institutional democracy. I reach out to the community because I want to contribute my part in effecting critical changes in larger society.

In service, I emphasize using my expertise to improve student learning. I review textbooks so that I can give students quality academic material to follow in their course work. I serve as an advisor for the Professional Sociological Students Association because I want to make myself available to our students for advice, from literature review, study skills, job search, and leadership to social advocacy. I invite prominent sociologists and experienced practitioners to my classes and department because I want to connect our students to the larger disciplinary community and the real world.

I emphasize offering my specialty to enhance the quality of scholarship and the unity of academic community. I spend hours to read papers for friends and colleagues in different institutions and disciplines so that I can offer them critical advice and comments to get their work published. I review manuscripts for publishers because I want to ensure that quality products are made available to the benefit of knowledge. I serve on graduate student advisory committees because I want to contribute my best in preparing qualified personnel for the work of scholarship.

I emphasize collegiality and professionalism in service. I serve on departmental, college, and university committees not because I want to seek the spotlight nor because I need to score points to offset an inadequate performance in teaching and research. I am disturbed to see junior faculty members misguided to engage in nominal, trivial, and unproductive service activities to the detriment of their vitally needed growth in teaching and research.

Service in the Department

A chronological list begins with the most recent.
(3) Coordinator, Affirmative Action (Equity & Diversity Representative), 2001-2009; 2009-2011

I remain in touch with appropriate agencies and authorities on and off campus; I gather policy documents, civil complaints, and litigation cases for possible faculty reference; I keep the faculty informed of equity issues in recruitment and hiring by alerting the faculty to the Affirmative Action Survey data on XXX applicants and making copies of the survey for the interested faculty; I review and sign off official documents for full-time faculty hiring and part-time faculty contract renewal from time to time.

Service in the College

A chronological list begins with the most recent.
(2) Cochair, Academic Planning Committee, 2007-2008
I work with the Cochair in scheduling committee meetings, preparing meeting agendas, screening proposals, communicating with department chairs/curriculum representatives/proposal authors, coordinating with curriculum-related agencies in the university, and presiding over committee meetings; I contribute thoughts and ideas at the meeting or via email on various issues pertaining to the work of the Committee; I review and evaluate curriculum proposals; I actively and constructively share my comments with other members of the Committee, helping shape the final decisions the Committee has to make on various course proposals from different departments in the College.

Service in the University

A chronological list begins with the most recent.
(5) Discipline Representative, Lower Division Transfer Project, 2004-2009

I attend statewide meetings for XXX, XXX, and XXX; I engage in heated debates on general education requirements, lower division courses, and transferable courses from community colleges; I propose, review, evaluate, and vote on various ideas; I make effective arguments for or against major proposals; I contribute to the final decision each discipline group has to make on its lower division transfer pattern, from XXX to XXX to XXX.

I consult with the Department Chair in the process; I review, evaluate, and give approval to the system-general lower division transfer pattern; I develop, fine-tune, and submit the campus-specific lower division transfer pattern; I respond to calls for report to the College, the University, and the Chancellor's Office; I identify and remain in touch with persons of contact from major community colleges feeding students to XXX, from XXX College to XXX College to the College of the XXX.

Acting as the discipline representative in the Lower Division Transfer Project is one of the most comprehensive, multifaceted, time-consuming, and long-lasting services I have performed in my academic career. Despite its enormous complexity, I serve it effectively and efficiently on behalf of my Discipline, Department, and University.

Service to the Community

A chronological list begins with the most recent.
(7) Member, XXX Advisory Board, XXX College, 2001-present

I attend regular meetings; I offer ideas, insights, and perspectives on issues ranging from program planning, curriculum design, student training and internship, faculty recruitment, candidate evaluation protocols, interview standards, and recent developments in XXX to the role of community college in larger academia; I am highly respected and well-liked by other members of the Board for my friendly, straightforward mannerism and my unique, insightful points of view.

My invited service at the community colleges not only bridges XXX with its feeder institutions in terms of student preparation and transferability, but also brings distinction to XXX as a local leader in teaching and scholarship.

Service to the Community: the Neighborhood, the District, and the Media

A chronological list begins with the most recent.

I routinely receive calls from the community for advice and comments on various specific issues, from problem kids in school to serial arsonists in the community and from teaching social studies in private school to applying grants with governmental agencies. I spend time searching and analyzing information from different sources and always answer questions in professional details.

My service in the neighborhood and over the local media not only connects XXX to its immediate social environment, but also brings distinction to XXX as an institution in the community and for the community.

Service to the Profession

My varied service to the profession manifests primarily in academic advisement, manuscript review, and conference organization.

Academic Advisement and Mentoring Activity

I serve on master and doctoral advisory committees for graduate students. For example, I worked closely with him for more than two years when I was on XXX's doctoral advisory committee at the University of XXX.

I remain in touch with and offer various advice or assistance to former XXX visiting scholars and foreign students after they return to their home countries. For example, I have provided a range of advice and support for Mr. XXX, a former visiting scholar on XXX International Exchange Program, since he left XXX to pursue his PhD in XXX.

I attend inquires and respond to requests for advice by students and scholars across the country and around the world who find me by my academic work. I carefully analyze their questions, search for academic references if necessary, and respond with technical details, especially to doctoral students in major research universities.

Manuscript and Grant Review

I am routinely invited by publishers, journals, and funding agencies to review manuscripts and grants. I respond to them because I want to ensure that serious academic research is supported and that quality scholarly products are made available to play their part in enhancing human understanding as well as in improving general social conditions.

In each review, I read the manuscript thoroughly; I make detailed comments throughout the manuscript; I write detailed comments on organization, coverage, writing, and other substantive matters; I make specific recommendations to the editor; I make constructive suggestions to the author(s). As applauded by the editors, my reviews are thoughtful, insightful, and reflective of most recent developments in the field.

Conference Organization and Service

I participate in professional conference organization in various roles as organizing member, translator, moderator, discussant, and chair because I want to ensure that scholars are connected in their research, that new ideas and methods are shared in a timely manner, and that knowledge grows and spreads through continuing communications across disciplines.

As session chair, I introduce speakers; provide thematic connections from presentation to presentation; I make critical comments on presentations; I take questions from the audience. With effective management, I ensure that sessions go smoothly and successfully in front of a highly active audience.

As session discussant, I collect papers from speakers before the meeting; I read each paper thoroughly; I make detailed comments on each paper; I provide thematic connections among presentations at the session. Through serious work, I ensure that both speakers and participants learn and contribute not only for the specific success of a session but also to the general benefit of scholarship.

As session organizer, I submit session proposals to the program committee; I receive, and solicit when necessary, papers from scholars in the field; I review and evaluate each submission; I send accepted papers to the program committee; I keep authors informed of the status of their submission as well as important dates pertaining to the meeting; I greet speakers personally at the meeting.

PROFESSIONAL AND PERSONAL RESPONSIBILITIES

I see myself a caring, honest, and responsible person. I fulfill my professional and personal responsibilities with commitment, devotion, and integrity as demonstrated in my academic pursuits and family life.

As a member of the teaching profession, I respect and take action to promote truth, quality, honesty, civility, academic standards, and freedom of inquiry. I learn from fellow members by studying their work, participating in academic seminars, and sitting in their classes. I contribute to the profession by publishing my research in pedagogy, presenting my papers to professional conferences, organizing sessions on teaching, reviewing textbooks, and offering advice to students across the country.

As a professor, I respect and take action to promote students' rights to knowledge, civil treatment, privacy, and academic freedom. I treat students as partners. I ask what they know before I teach them what they do not know. I work on educational access to students. I work to create a friendly learning environment for students. I connect students to the real world. I foster self-confidence in students. I teach students not only substance in a subject, but also essential skills in study and job functioning. I care about what students have learned and how they feel about their learning. My unassuming teaching style, my caring attitude, and my effort to create a facilitative learning environment are well received by students as reflected in comments from officially administered anonymous student evaluations.

As a colleague, I respect and take action to promote collegiality, professionalism, academic autonomy, and freedom of inquiry. Specifically, I follow three principles in my relationships with colleagues. First, be modest and appreciative, and always learn from colleagues. I sit in their classes, read their work, seek their advice, and learn from them in every possible occasion. Second, be collegial and respectful, and never feel enough in attending to colleagues on their needs and inquiries. I work with them on committees. I attend to their inquiries in a timely and professional manner. I read their papers and offer them comments when appropriate. I share with them information I gather from the outside. I share with them my experiences in teaching, research, and service. Third, be gracious and grateful, and never feel enough in supporting colleagues in their professional endeavors. I appreciate what I have learned from my colleagues. I am deeply grateful when some of my colleagues kindly write to me: "You are a bright and industrious young colleague, and I am so glad we have you as part of our department, as well as a friend!" and "... and I were discussing ... and we both said that the department is lucky to have you, since you are so excellent in theory as well as other areas." I look forward to the opportunity to support my colleagues in all of their academic pursuits.

As a member of the institution, I take what I characterize as a family approach. I treat myself as a family member. I not only work conscientiously to fulfill all my responsibilities, but also care about the welfare of other family members and the reputation of the whole family. I ask myself in everything I do: Do I bring any honor to my family? Specifically, I work passionately with students inside and outside the classroom because I know if they are not satisfied with my teaching they will feel negative about my department, my college, and my university. I work painstakingly on research and publication because I know if I do not publish or publish low-quality products it will to some degree reflect unfavorably on my department, my college, and my university. I respond to service requests from the community and the profession because I know if I do not act properly and professionally it will have an adverse impact on my department, my college, and my university. The reputation of an academic institution lies directly in its quality of teaching, its productivity in research, and its response to community needs. As a member of the institution, I have an inalienable responsibility to do my part in enhancing its general reputation in the larger society.

REFERENCES

Abdelal, R., Herrera, Y., Johnston, A. I., & McDermott, R. (2009). *Measuring identity: A guide for social scientists.* New York, NY: Cambridge University Press.

Abel, E. K. (1984). *Terminal degrees: The job crisis in higher education.* New York, NY: Praeger.

Ackerman, J. M., & Coogan, D. J. (2010). *The public work of rhetoric: Citizen-scholars and civic engagement.* Columbia, SC: University of South Carolina Press.

Aldridge, J., & Derrington, A. M. (2012). *The research funding toolkit: How to plan and write successful grant applications.* Thousand Oaks, CA: SAGE.

Alstete, J. W. (2000). *Posttenure faculty development: Building a system for faculty improvement and appreciation.* San Francisco, CA: Jossey-Bass.

Altbach, P. G., Gumport, P. J., Berdahl, R. O. (2011). *American higher education in the twenty-first century: Social, political, and economic challenges.* Baltimore, MD: The Johns Hopkins University Press.

Anastas, J. W. (2012). *Doctoral education in social work.* New York, NY: Oxford University Press.

Axelrod, B., & Windell, J. (2012). *Dissertation solutions: A concise guide to planning, implementing, and surviving your doctoral project.* Lanham, MD: R&L Education.

Azzarello, P., & Ferrazzi, K. (2012). *Rise: 3 practical steps for advancing your career, standing out as a leader, and liking your life.* New York, NY: Ten Speed Press.

Baez, B. (2002). *Affirmative action, hate speech, and tenure: Narratives about race, law, and the academy.* New York, NY: Routledge Falmer.

Bain, K. (2004). *What the best college teachers do.* Cambridge, MA: Harvard University Press.

Baldwin, R. G., & Chronister, J. L. (2001). *Teaching without tenure: Policies and practices for a new era.* Baltimore, MD: Johns Hopkins University Press.

Barnard, M. (1990). *Magazine and journal production.* New York, NY: Van Nostrand Reinhold.

Barnes, S. L. (2007). *On the market: Strategies for a successful academic job search.* Boulder, CO: Lynne Rienner.

Baudrillard, J. (1988). *Selected writings* (M. Poster, Ed.). Palo Alto, CA: Stanford University Press.

Bauer, D. G. (1999). *The "how to" grants manual: Successful grant-seeking techniques for obtaining public and private grants.* Phoenix, AZ: Oryx Press.

Becker, H. S. (1998). *Tricks of the trade: How to think about your research while you're doing it.* Chicago, IL: The University of Chicago Press.

Beckham, J. (1986). *Faculty/staff nonrenewal and dismissal for cause in institutions of higher education.* Asheville, NC: College Administration Publications.

Belcher, W. L. (2009). *Writing your journal article in twelve weeks: A guide to academic publishing success.* Thousand Oaks, CA: SAGE.

Bentley, P. J., Coates, H., Dobson, I. R., Goedegebuure, L., & Meek, V. L. (2013). *Job satisfaction around the academic world.* New York, NY: Springer.

Berkun, S. (2010). *Confessions of a public speaker.* Sebastopol, CA: O'Reilly Media.

Bianco-Mathis, V., & Chalofsky, N. (1999). *The full-time faculty handbook.* Thousand Oaks, CA: SAGE.

Bland, C. J., Taylor, A. L., Shollen, S. L., Weber-Main, A. M., & Mulcahy, P. A. (2009). *Faculty success through mentoring: A guide for mentors, mentees, and leaders.* Lanham, MD: Rowman & Littlefield.

Blaxter, L., Hughes, C., & Tight, M. (1998). *The academic career handbook.* Philadelphia, PA: Open University Press.

Bok, D. (2003). *Universities in the marketplace: Commercialization of higher education.* Princeton, NJ: Princeton University Press.

Bolek, C. S., Bielawski, L., Niemcryk, S., Needle, R., & Baker, S. (1992). Developing a competitive research proposal. *Drugs and Society, 6*(1/2), 1-22.

Bolker, J. (1998). *Writing your dissertation in fifteen minutes a day: A guide to starting, revising, and finishing your doctoral thesis.* New York, NY: Henry Holt.

Bolman, L. G., & Gallos, J. V. (2011). *Reframing academic leadership.* San Francisco, CA: Jossey-Bass.

Bowen, W. G., & Rudenstine, N. L. (1992). *In pursuit of the PhD.* Princeton, NJ: Princeton University Press.

Bowen, W. G., & Sosa, J. A. (1989). *Prospects for faculty in the arts and sciences: A study of factors affecting demand and supply, 1987 to 2012.* Princeton, NJ: Princeton University Press.

Brada, J. C., Stanley, G., & Bienkowski, W. (2012). *The university in the age of globalization: Rankings, resources and reforms.* New York, NY: Palgrave Macmillan.

Bright, D. F., & Richards, M. P. (2001). *The academic deanship: Individual careers and institutional roles.* San Francisco, CA: Jossey-Bass.

Brodkey, L. (1987). *Academic writing as social practice.* Philadelphia, PA: Temple University Press.

Brown, D., & Brooks, L. 1996. *Career choice and development.* San Francisco, CA: Jossey-Bass.

Brown-Glaude, W. (2008). *Doing diversity in higher education: Faculty leaders share challenges and strategies.* New Brunswick, NJ: Rutgers University Press.

Buller, J. L. (2010). *The essential college professor: A practical guide to an academic career.* San Francisco, CA: Jossey-Bass.

Buller, J. L. (2012). *Best practices in faculty evaluation: A practical guide for academic leaders.* San Francisco, CA: Jossey-Bass.

Busch, F. (1986). *When people publish: Essays on writers and writing.* Iowa City, IA: University of Iowa Press.

Butin, D. W. (2010). *The education dissertation: A guide for practitioner scholars.* Thousand Oaks, CA: Corwin Press.

Cain, T. R. (2012). *Establishing academic freedom: Politics, principles, and the development of core values*. New York, NY: Palgrave Macmillan.

Cantor, J. A. (1993). *A guide to academic writing*. Westport, CT: Greenwood Press.

Carrigan, D. P. (1991). Publish or perish: The troubled state of scholarly communication. *Scholarly Publishing, 22*(3), 131-142.

Cartter, A. M. (1976). *Ph.D.'s and the academic labor market*. New York, NY: McGraw Hill.

Caughey, J. L. (2006). *Negotiating cultures and identities: Life history issues, methods, and readings*. Lincoln, NE: University of Nebraska Press.

Chait, R. P. (2005). *The question of tenure*. Cambridge, MA: Harvard University Press.

Chu, D. (2012). *The department chair primer: What chairs need to know and do to make a difference*. San Francisco, CA: Jossey-Bass.

Cion, J. Frey, C., Sorskin, C., & Sevick, R. (2012). *Nonprofit governance and management*. Chicago, IL: American Bar Association.

Clark, C., Fasching-Varner, K., & Brimhall-Vargas, M. (2012). *Occupying the academy: Just how important is diversity work in higher education?* Lanham, MD: Rowman & Littlefield.

Clark, M. J., & Centra, J. A. (1985). Influences on the career accomplishments of PhD's. *Research in Higher Education, 23*(3), 256-269.

Clark, S. M., & Lewis, D. R. (1985). *Faculty vitality and institutional productivity: Critical perspectives for higher education*. New York, NY: Teachers College Press.

Clark, W. (2006). *Academic charisma and the origins of the research university*. Chicago, IL: The University of Chicago Press.

Coerver, H., & Byers, M. (2011). *Race for relevance: 5 radical changes for associations*. Washington, DC: American Society of Association Executives.

Cohen, S. (1997). Conference life: The rough guide. *The American sociologist, 28*(3), 69-84.

Coiner, C., & George, D. H. (1998). *The family track: Keeping your faculties while you mentor, nurture, teach, and serve*. Chicago, IL: University of Illinois Press.

Coley, S. M., & Scheinberg, C. A. (2008). *Proposal writing: Effective grantsmanship*. Thousand Oaks, CA: SAGE.

Conley, V. M. (1997). *Characteristics and attitudes of instructional faculty and staff in the humanities*. Washington, DC: U.S. Department of Education.

Coser, L. A., Kadushin, C., & Powell, W. W. (1982). *The culture and commerce of publishing*. New York, NY: Basic Books.

Cotten, S. R., Price, J., Keeton, S., Burton, R. P. D., & Wittekind, J. E. C. (2001). Reflections on the academic job search in sociology. *The American Sociologist, 32*(3), 26-42.

Cownie, F. (2004). *Legal academics: Culture and identities*. Portland, OR: Hart.

Cox, J. B. (2007). *Professional practices in association management: The essential resource for effective management of nonprofit organizations*. Washington, DC: ASAE & The Center for Association Leadership.

Cox, J., & Cox, L. (2006). *Scholarly publishing practice*. Brighton, England: Association of Learned and Professional Society.

Crookston, R. K. (2012). *Working with problem faculty: A six-step guide for department chairs*. San Francisco, CA: Jossey-Bass.

Cyr, D., & Reich, B. H. (1996). *Scaling the ivory tower: Stories from women in business school faculties*. Westport, CT: Praeger.

Dalton, J., & Dignam, M. (2007). *The decision to join: How individuals determine value and why they choose to belong*. Washington, DC: Association Management Press.

Darling, D. (2005). *Networking for career success*. New York, NY: McGraw-Hill

Davis, G. B., & Parker, C. A. (1997). *Writing the doctoral dissertation: A systematic approach*. Hauppauge, NY: Barron's Educational Series.

De George, R. T. (1997). *Academic freedom and tenure: Ethical issues*. Lanham, MD: Rowman & Littlefield.

Deely, J. N. (2001). *Four ages of understanding: The first postmodern survey of philosophy from ancient times to the turn of the twenty-first century*. Toronto, Canada: University of Toronto Press.

Dews, C. L. B., & Law, C. L. Eds. (1995). *This fine place so far from home: Voices of academics from the working class*. Philadelphia, PA: Temple University Press.

Dewsbury, D. A. (1996). *Unification through division: Histories of the divisions of the American Psychological Association*. Washington, DC: American Psychological Association.

Di Leo, J. R. (2003). *Affiliations: Identity in academic culture*. Lincoln, NE: University of Nebraska Press.

Dickeson, R. C. (1999). *Prioritizing academic programs and services: Reallocating resources to achieve strategic balance*. San Francisco, CA: Jossey-Bass.

Digiusto, E. (1994). Equity in authorship: A strategy for assigning credit when publishing. *Social Science and Medicine, 38*(1), 55-58.

Dobson, J. (2010). *Death without tenure: A professor Karen Pelletier mystery*. Scottsdale, AZ: Poisoned Pen Press.

Doherty, P. (2008). *The beginner's guide to winning the Nobel Prize: Advice for young scientists*. New York, NY: Columbia University Press.

Dore, R. P. (1976). *The diploma disease: Education, qualification, and development*. Berkeley, CA: University of California Press.

Dulmus, C. N., & Sowers, K. M. (2012). *The profession of social work: Guided by history, led by evidence*. Hoboken, NJ: John Wiley & Sons.

Editorial Board. (1993). *The awards almanac*. Chicago, IL: St. James Press.

Elliott, A. (1996). *Subject to ourselves*. Cambridge, MA: Blackwell.

Ellis, E. M. (2001). The impact of race and gender on graduate school socialization, satisfaction with doctoral study, and commitment to degree completion. *The Western Journal of Black Studies, 25*(1), 30-45.

English, J. F. (2005). *The economy of prestige: Prizes, awards, and the circulation of cultural value*. Cambridge, MA: Harvard University Press.

Engvall, R. P. (2003). *Academic identity: Place, race, and gender in academia*. Cresskill, NJ: Hampton Press.

Eurich, N. (1981). *Systems of higher education in twelve countries: A comparative view*. New York, NY: Praeger.

Fabricant, F., Miller, J., & Stark, D. (2013). *Creating career success: A flexible plan for the world of work*. Belmont, CA: Wadsworth.

Fairweather, J. S. (1996). *Faculty work and public trust: Restoring the value of teaching and public service in American academic life*. Boston, MA: Allyn & Bacon.

Feldman, B. (2011). *The Nobel Prize: A history of genius, controversy, and prestige*. New York, NY: Arcade.

Feldman, D. (2013). *Managing careers*. New York, NY: Routledge.

Fenton, N., Bryman, A., Deacon, D., & Birmingham, P. (1997). Sod off and find us a boffin: Journalists and the social science conference. *The Sociological Review, 45*(1), 1-23.

Finkelstein, M. J. (1984). *The American academic profession: A synthesis of social scientific inquiry since World War II*. Columbus, OH: Ohio State University Press.

Finkelstein, M. J., Seal, R. K., & Schuster, J. H. (1998). *The new academic generation: A profession in transformation*. Baltimore, MD: The Johns Hopkins University Press.

Finkin, M. W. (1996). *The case for tenure*. Ithaca, NY: ILR Press.

Flemons, D. G. (1998). *Writing between the lines: Composition in the social sciences*. New York, NY: W. W. Norton.

Formo, D. M., & Reed, C. (2011). *Job Search in academe: How to get the position you deserve*. Sterling, VA: Stylus.

Fox, M. F. (1985). *Scholarly writing and publishing: Issues, problems, and solutions*. Boulder, CO: Westview Press.

Garber, M. B. (2001). *Academic instincts*. Princeton, NJ: Princeton University Press.

Gardner, J. N., & Barefoot, B. O. (2010). *Step by step to college and career success*. New York, NY: Bedford/St. Martin's.

Gardner, S. K., & Mendoza. P. (2010). *On becoming a scholar: Socialization and development in doctoral education*. Sterling, VA: Stylus.

Garfinkle, J. A. (2011). *Getting ahead: Three steps to take your career to the next level*. Hoboken, NJ: John Wiley & Sons.

Goffman, E. (1959). *The presentation of self in everyday life*. Garden City, NY: Doubleday.

Golde, C. M., & Walker, G. E. (2006). *Envisioning the future of doctoral education: Preparing the stewards of the discipline*. San Francisco, CA: Jossey-Bass/Carnegie Foundation for the Advancement of Teaching.

Goldsmith, J. A., Komlos, J., & Gold, P. S. (2001). *The Chicago guide to your academic career: A portable mentor for scholars from graduate school through tenure*. Chicago, IL: The University of Chicago Press.

Gornitzka, A., Kogan, M., & Amaral, A. (2007). *Reform and change in higher education: Analyzing policy implementation*. New York, NY: Springer/Consortium of Higher Education Researchers.

Gosling, P. A., & Noordam, B. D. (2006). *Mastering your PhD: Survival and success in the doctoral years and beyond*. New York, NY: Springer.

Gossett, J. L., & Bellas, M. L. (2002). You can't put a rule around people's hearts … can you? Consensual relationship policies in academia. *Sociological Focus, 35*(3), 267-284.

Gould, R. (1978). *Transformations: Growth and change in adult life*. New York, NY: Simon & Schuster.

Graham, S., Emery, S., & Hall. R. (2012). *Identity: Your passport to success*. Upper Saddle River, NJ: FT Press.

Grant, W., & Sherrington, P. (2006). *Managing your academic careers*. Hampshire, England: Palgrave Macmillan.

Gray, P., & Drew, D. E. (2008). *What they didn't teach you in graduate school: 199 help-ful hints for success in your academic career.* Sterling, VA: Stylus.

Greenwood, D., & Levin, M. (2001). Re-organizing universities and "Knowing How": University restructuring and knowledge creation for the 21st century. *Organization, 8*(2), 433-440.

Halvorsen, T., & Nyhagen, A. (2011). *Academic identities—Academic challenges? American and European experience of the transformation of higher education and research.* Newcastle upon Tyne, England: Cambridge Scholars.

Hamilton, N. W. (2002). *Academic ethics: Problems and materials on professional conduct and shared governance.* Westport, CT: Praeger/American Council on Education.

Haskell, T. L. (2000). *The emergence of professional social science: The American Social Science Association and the nineteenth-century crisis of authority.* Baltimore, MD: The Johns Hopkins University Press.

Heiberger, M. M., & Vick, J. M. (2001). *The academic job search handbook.* Philadel-phia: PA: University of Pennsylvania Press.

Heinz, W. R., & Marshall, V. W. (2003). *Social dynamics of the life course: Transitions, institutions, and interrelations.* Hawthorne, NY: Aldine de Gruyter.

Henson, K. T. (2004). *Writing for publication: Road to academic advancement.* Boston, MA: Allyn & Bacon.

Hermanowicz, J. C. (2002). In the shadows of giants: Identity and institution building in the American academic profession. In R. A. Settersten & T. J. Owens (Eds.), *Advances in life course research: New frontiers in socialization* (pp. 133-162). Oxford, England: JAI.

Hermanowicz, J. C. (2012). *Lives in science: How institutions affect academic careers.* Chicago, IL: The University of Chicago Press.

Holden, C. (1991). Do we need more PhDs, or is fewer really better? *Science, 251*(4997), 1017-1018.

Holland, K., & Watson, R. (2012). *Writing for publication in nursing and healthcare.* Ames, IA: Wiley-Blackwell.

Holley, K. A. (2011). A cultural repertoire of practices in doctoral education. *International Journal of Doctoral Studies, 6,* 79-94.

Huer, J. (1991). *Tenure for Socrates: A study in the betrayal of the American professor.* New York, NY: Bergin & Garvey.

Hume, K. (2010). *Surviving your academic job hunt: Advice for humanities PhDs.* New York, NY: Palgrave Macmillan.

Hunt, D. D. (2012). *The new nurse educator: Mastering academe.* New York, NY: Springer.

Hyland, K. (2006). *English for academic purposes: An advanced resource book.* New York, NY: Routledge.

Jacobs, S., & Assante, C. (2008). *Membership essentials: Recruitment, retention, roles, responsibilities, and resources.* Washington, DC: American Society of Association Executives.

Jedding, K. (2010). *Higher education: On life, landing a job, and everything else they didn't teach you in college.* New York, NY: Rodale Books.

Joughin, L. (1967). *Academic freedom and tenure: A handbook of the American Association of University Professors.* Madison, WI: University of Wisconsin Press.

Kalman, C. S. (2007). *Successful science and engineering teaching in colleges and universities.* Bolton, MA: Anker.

Karsh, E., & Fox, A. S. (2009). *The only grant-writing book you'll ever need.* New York, NY3: Basic Books.

Kinnick, M. K. (1994). *Providing useful information for deans and department chairs.* San Francisco, CA: Jossey-Bass.

Kitchin, R., & Fuller, D. (2005). *The academic's guide to publishing.* Thousand Oaks, CA: SAGE.

Lang, J. M. (2010). *On course: A week-by-week guide to your first semester of college teaching.* Cambridge, MA: Harvard University Press.

Lattuca, L. R. (2001). *Creating interdisciplinarity: Interdisciplinary research and teaching among college and university faculty.* Nashville, TN: Vanderbilt University Press.

Leaming, D. R. (2003). *Managing people: A guide for department chairs and deans.* San Francisco, CA: Jossey-Bass.

Leap, T. L. (1995). *Tenure, discrimination, and the courts.* Ithaca, NY: ILR Press.

Ledoux, M. W., Wilhite, S. C., & Silver, P. F. (2011). *Civic engagement and service learning in a metropolitan university: Multiple approaches and perspectives.* Hauppauge, NY: Nova Science.

Lee, A., & Danby, S. (2012). *Reshaping doctoral education: International approaches and pedagogies.* New York, NY: Routledge.

Levinson, D. J. (1978). *The seasons of a man's life.* New York, NY: Ballantine Books.

Lewis, M. (1997). *Poisoning the ivy: The seven deadly sins and other vices of higher education in America.* Armonk, NY: M. E. Sharpe.

Li, P., & Marrongelle, K. (2012). *Having success with NSF: A practical guide.* Ames, IA: Wiley-Blackwell.

Licata, C. M. (1986). *Post-tenure faculty evaluation: Threat or opportunity?* Washington, DC: Association for the Study of Higher Education.

Lindholm-Romantschuk, Y. (1998). *Scholarly book reviewing in the social sciences and humanities: The flow of ideas within and among disciplines.* Westport, CT: Greenwood Press.

Locke, L. F., Spirduso, W. W., & Silverman, S. J. (2013). *Proposals that work: A guide for planning dissertations and grant proposals.* Thousand Oaks, CA: SAGE.

Long, J. S., McGinnis, R., & Allison, P. D. (1993). Rank advancement in academic careers: Sex differences and the effects of productivity. *American Sociological Review, 58*(5), 703-722.

Lucas, A. F. (2000). *Leading academic change: Essential roles for department chairs.* San Francisco, CA: Jossey-Bass.

Lyson, T. A., & Squires, G. D. (1978). The new academic hustle: Marketing a PhD *The American Sociologist, 13*(4), 233-238.

MacDonald, S. (1994). *Professional academic writing in the humanities and social sciences.* Carbondale & Edwardsville, IL: Southern Illinois University Press.

Macfarlane, B. (2007). *The academic citizen: The virtue of service in university life.* New York, NY: Routledge.

Macfarlane, B. (2012). *Intellectual leadership in higher education: Renewing the role of the university professor.* New York, NY: Routledge.

Maki, P. L., & Borkowski, N. A. (2006). *The assessment of doctoral education: Emerging criteria and new models for improving outcomes*. Sterling, VA: Stylus.

Marx, K. (1967). *Capital* (S. Moore & E. Aveling, Trans.). New York, NY: International.

Maslow, A. H. (1954). *Motivation and personality*. New York, NY: Harper.

McAlpine, L., & Akerlind, G. (2010). *Becoming an academic: An international perspective*. New York, NY: Palgrave Macmillan.

McAlpine, L. & Amundsen, C. (2011). *Doctoral education: Research-based strategies for doctoral students, supervisors and administrators*. New York, NY: Springer.

McCabe, L. L., & McCabe, E. R. B. (2010). *How to succeed in academics*. Berkeley, CA: University of California Press.

McCaffery, P. (2010). *The higher education manager's handbook: Effective leadership and management in universities and colleges*. New York, NY: Routledge.

McGinty, S. (1999). *Gatekeepers of knowledge: Journal editors in the sciences and the social sciences*. Westport, CT: Bergin & Garvey.

McKinney, K. (2013). *The scholarship of teaching and learning in and across the disciplines*. Bloomington, IN: Indiana University Press.

Meiners, Roger E. 2004. *Faculty towers: Tenure and the structure of higher education*. Oakland, CA: Independent Institute.

Meyers, M. (2012). *Prize fight: The race and the rivalry to be the first in science*. New York, NY: Palgrave Macmillan.

Miedaner, T. (2010). *Coach yourself to a new career: 7 steps to reinventing your professional life*. New York, NY: McGraw Hill.

Misner, I., Alexander, D., & Hilliard, B. (2009). *Networking like a pro: Turning contacts into connections*. Irvine, CA: Entrepreneur Press.

Mullen, C. A. (2012). *From student to professor: Translating a graduate degree into a career in academia*. Lanham, MD: R&L Education.

Nealon, J. (2012). *Post-postmodernism: Or, the cultural logic of just-in-time capitalism*. Stanford, CA: Stanford University Press.

Newman, F., Couturier, L., & Scurry, J. (2004). *The future of higher education: Rhetoric, reality, and the risk of the market*. San Francisco, CA: Jossey-Bass.

Nilson, L. B. (2010). *Teaching at its best: A research-based resource for college instructors*. San Francisco, CA: Jossey-Bass.

Noble, K. A. (1994). *Changing doctoral degrees: An international perspective*. Bristol, PA: Open University Press.

Norrby, E. (2010). *Nobel prizes and life sciences*. Singapore: World Scientific Publishing.

Orlich, D. C., & Shrope, N. R. (2012). *Developing a winning grant proposal*. New York, NY: Routledge.

Paechter, C. (2001). *Knowledge, power, and learning*. Thousand Oaks, CA: SAGE.

Pappas, J. P., & Jerman, J. (2011). *Meeting adult learner needs through the nontraditional doctoral degree: New directions for adult and continuing education*. San Francisco, CA: Jossey-Bass.

Parsons, P. (1989). *Getting published: The acquisition process at university presses*. Knoxville, TN: University of Tennessee Press.

Peck, R. M., & Stroud, P. T. (2012). *A glorious enterprise: The Academy of Natural Sciences of Philadelphia and the making of American science*. Philadelphia, PA: University of Pennsylvania Press.

Perlmutter, D. D. (2010). *Promotion and tenure confidential*. Cambridge, MA: Harvard University Press.

Philipsen, M. I. (2008). *Challenges of the faculty career for women: Success and sacrifice*. San Francisco, CA: Jossey-Bass.

Piper, D. W. (1992). Are professors professional? *Higher Education Quarterly, 46*(2), 145-156.

Popkewitz, T. S., & Fendler, L. (1999). *Critical theories in education: Changing terrains of knowledge and politics*. New York, NY: Routledge.

Porter, S. E. (2010). *Inking the deal: A guide for successful academic publishing*. Waco, TX: Baylor University Press.

Powell, W. W. (1985. *Getting into print: The decision-making process in scholarly publishing*. Chicago, IL: The University of Chicago Press.

Pratt, D. (2007). *The impossible takes longer: The 1,000 wisest things ever said by Nobel Prize laureates*. New York, NY: Walker.

Professional Convention Management Association. (2006). *Professional meeting management: Comprehensive strategies for meetings, conventions, and events*. Dubuque, IA: Kendall/Hunt.

Rajagopal, I., & Lin, Z. (1996). Hidden careerists in Canadian universities. *Higher Education, 32*(3), 247-266

Readings, B. (1996). *The university in ruins*. Cambridge, MA: Harvard University Press.

Reinhart, S. M. (2002). *Giving academic presentations*. Ann Arbor, MI: University of Michigan Press.

Rendle-Short, J. (2006). *The Academic presentation: Situated talk in action*. Burlington, VT: Ashgate.

Reynolds, G. (2012). *Presentation zen: Simple ideas on presentation design and delivery*. Berkeley, CA: New Riders Press.

Rhode, D. (2006). *In pursuit of knowledge: Scholars, status, and academic culture*. Stanford, CA: Stanford University Press.

Rhodes, F. H. T. (2001). *The creation of the future: The role of the American university*. Ithaca, NY: Cornell University Press.

Ries, J. B., & Leukefeld, C. G. (1995). *Applying for research funding: Getting started and getting funded*. Thousand Oaks, CA: SAGE.

Rocco, T. S., Hatcher, T., & Creswell, J. W. (2011). *The handbook of scholarly writing and publishing*. San Francisco, CA: Jossey-Bass.

Rockquemore, K. A., & Laszloffy, T. 2008. *The Black academic's guide to winning tenure—Without losing your soul*. Boulder, CO: Lynne Rienner.

Rodmann, D. (1995). *Career transitions for chemists*. Washington, DC: American Chemical Society.

Rosenwasser, D., & Stephen, J. (1997). *Writing analytically*. Fort Worth, TX: Harcourt Brace College.

Rossides, D. W. (1998). *Professions and disciplines: Functional and conflict perspectives*. Upper Saddle River, NJ: Prentice Hall.

Sachs, M. (1990). *World guide to scientific associations and learned societies*. New York, NY: K.G. Saur.

Savage, J. D. (2000). *Funding science in America: Congress, universities, and the politics of the academic pork barrel*. New York, NY: Cambridge University Press.

Schuster, J. H., & Finkelstein, M. J. (2006). *The American faculty: The restructuring of academic work and careers*. Baltimore, MD: The Johns Hopkins University Press.

Seldin, P. (2007). *The teaching portfolio: A practical guide to improved performance and promotion/tenure decisions*. San Francisco, CA: Jossey-Bass.

Shattock, M. (2003). *Managing successful universities*. Berkshire, England: Open University Press/Society for Research into Higher Education.

Shaw, V. N. (1999). Reading, presentation, and writing skills in content courses. *College Teaching, 47*(4), 153-157.

Shaw, V. N. (2000). Toward professional civility: An analysis of rejection letters from sociology departments. *The American Sociologist, 31*(1), 32-43.

Shaw, V. N. (2001a). Training in reading skills: An innovative method from classroom instruction. *Reading Improvement, 38*(4), 188-192.

Shaw, V. N. (2001b). Self-dialogue as a fundamental process of expression. *Social Thought and Research, 24*(1/2), 271-312.

Shaw, V. N. (2001c). Training in presentation skills: An innovative method from classroom instruction. *Education, 122*(1), 140-144.

Shaw, V. N. (2002a). Peer review as a motivating device in the training of writing skills for college students. *Journal of College Reading and Learning, 33*(1), 68-76.

Shaw, V. N. (2002b). Counseling the university professor on the securing of research grants and the publishing of research products. *Education, 123*(2), 395-400.

Shaw, V. N. (2002c). Essential social sciences skills in college and university education. *Contemporary Education, 72*(1), 39-43.

Shaw, V. N. (2009). Scholarly publishing: Reforms for user friendliness and system efficiency. *Journal of Scholarly Publishing, 40*(3), 241-262.

Shoenfeld, C., & Magnan, R. (2004). *Mentor in a manual: Climbing the academic ladder to tenure*. Madison, WI: Atwood Publications.

Shore, A. R., & Carfora, J. M. (2011). *The art of funding and implementing ideas: A guide to proposal development and project management*. Thousand Oaks, CA: SAGE.

Silverman, F. H. (2001). *Publishing for tenure and beyond: Strategies for maximizing your student ratings*. Westport, CT: Bergin & Garvey.

Sladek, S. L. (2011). *The end of membership as we know it: Building the fortune-flipping, must-have association of the next century*. Washington, DC: ASAE/Center for Association Leadership.

Slaughter, S., & Rhoades, G. (2004). *Academic capitalism and the new economy: Markets, state, and higher education*. Baltimore, MD: The Johns Hopkins University Press.

Smith, B. L. (1973). *The tenure debate*. San Francisco, CA: Jossey Bass.

Sowers-Hoag, K., & Harrison, D. F. 1998. *Finding an academic job*. Thousand Oaks, CA: SAGE.

St. John, E. P., & Parsons, M. D. (2004). *Public funding of higher education: Changing contexts and new rationales*. Baltimore, MD: The Johns Hopkins University Press.

Stinchcombe, A. L. (1999/2000). Making a living in sociology in the 21st century (and the intellectual consequences of making a living). *Berkeley Journal of Sociology, 44*, 4-14.

Svinicki, M., & McKeachie, W. J. (2011). *McKeachie's teaching tips: Strategies, research, and theory for college and university teachers*. Belmont, CA: Wadsworth.

Sweet, S. (1998). Practicing radical pedagogy: Balancing ideals with institutional constraints. *Teaching Sociology, 26*(2), 100-111.

Talburt, S. (2000). *Subject to identity: Knowledge, sexuality, and academic practices in higher education*. Albany, NY: State University of New York Press.

Taylor, S. (2005). *A handbook for doctoral supervisors*. New York, NY: Routledge.

Thelin, J. R. (2011). *A history of American higher education*. Baltimore, MD: The Johns Hopkins University Press.

Thomson, P., & Walker, M. (2010). *The Routledge doctoral students companion: Getting to grips with research in education and the social sciences*. New York, NY: Routledge.

Tierney, W. G. (1997). Organizational socialization in higher education. *Journal of Higher Education, 68*(1), 1-16.

Tierney, W. G. (2004). *Competing conceptions of academic governance: Negotiating the perfect storm*. Baltimore, MD: The Johns Hopkins University Press.

Tierney, W. G. (2006). *Governance and the public good*. Albany, NY: State University of New York Press.

Tierney, W. G., & Bensimon, E. M. (1996). *Promotion and tenure: Community and socialization in academe*. Albany, NY: State University of New York Press.

Tinkler, P., & Jackson, C. (2004). *The doctoral examination process*. Berkshire, England: Open University Press.

Tomlinson, M. (2013). *Education, work and identity: Themes and perspectives*. New York, NY: Continuum.

Toren, N., & Moore, D. (1998). The academic "hurdle race": A case study. *Higher Education, 35*(3), 267-283

Tuckman, H. P., Coyle, S., & Bae, Y. (1990). *On time to the doctorate: A study of the increased time to complete doctorates in science and engineering*. Washington, DC: National Academy Press.

Van Fraassen, B. C. (2010). *Scientific representation: Paradoxes of perspective*. Oxford, England: Oxford University Press.

VanZanten, S. (2011). *Joining the mission: A guide for (mainly) new college faculty*. Grand Rapids, MI: Eerdmans.

Vick, J. M., & Furlong, J. S. (2008). *The academic job search handbook*. Philadelphia, PA: University of Pennsylvania Press.

Walker, G. E., Golde, C. M., Jones, L., Bueschel, A. C., & Hutchings, P. (2008). *The formation of scholars: Rethinking doctoral education for the twenty-first century*. San Francisco, CA: Jossey-Bass/Carnegie Foundation for the Advancement of Teaching.

Walshaw, M. (2012). *Getting to grips with doctoral research*. New York, NY: Palgrave Macmillan.

Wasserman, P., & McLean, J. W. (1978). *Awards, honors, and prizes*. Detroit, MI: Gale Research.

Webb, A. (2009). *The doctoral degree in English education*. Kennesaw, GA: Kennesaw State University Press.

Weber, M. (1930). *The protestant ethic and the rise of capitalism*. New York, NY: Scribner.

Weddle, P. (2007). *2007/8 guide to association websites*. Stamford, CT: Weddle's.

Weingartner, R. H. (1999). *The moral dimensions of academic administration*. Lanham, MD: Rowman & Littlefield.

Weingartner, R. H. (2011). *Fitting form to function: A primer on the organization of academic institutions*. Lanham, MD: Rowman & Littlefield.

Weissman, J. (2011). *Presentations in action: 80 memorable presentation lessons from the masters*. Upper Saddle River, NJ: FT Press.

Whitchurch, C., & Gordon, G. (2010). *Academic and professional identities in higher education: The challenges of a diversifying workforce*. New York, NY: Routledge.

White, V. (1983). *Grant proposals that succeeded*. New York, NY: Plenum Press.

Wildavsky, A. B. (1989). *Craftways: On the organization of scholarly work*. New Brunswick, NJ: Transaction.

Young, M. L. (1985). *Scientific and technical organizations and agencies directory*. Detroit, MI: Gale Research.

Young, S., & Shaw, D. G. (1999). Profiles of effective college and university teachers. *Journal of Higher Education, 70*(6), 670-686.

ABOUT THE AUTHOR

Victor N. Shaw, PhD, is a professor of sociology at California State University-Northridge. Dr. Shaw is interested in the study of crime, deviance, social control, organizational behavior, higher education, academic careers, and public policy, and has published widely in those areas. One of Dr. Shaw's books, *Substance Use and Abuse: Sociological Perspectives*, appeared in "Outstanding Academic Titles," *CHOICE: Current Reviews for Academic Libraries*, the Association of College and Research Libraries.

CPSIA information can be obtained at www.ICGtesting.com
Printed in the USA
LVOW10s0058120514

385282LV00001B/68/P